LANDSCAPE-GARDENING

O. C. SIMONDS

As a 3rd generation - Best wishes
Robert C. Simonds
1-3-2002

Introduction by Robert E. Grese

Robert E. Grese

University of Massachusetts Press

AMHERST

in association with

Library of American Landscape History

AMHERST

This volume is reprinted from the first edition of *Landscape-Gardening*,
published by The Macmillan Company in 1920.

Printed in the United States of America
LC 00-028215
ISBN 1-55849-258-5
Printed and bound by Sheridan Books, Inc.

Library of Congress Cataloging-in-Publication Data
Simonds, Ossian Cole, 1855-1931
Landscape-gardening / O.C. Simonds ; introduction by Robert E. Grese.
p. cm.
Originally published: New York : The Macmillan Company, 1920. With new introd.
ISBN 1-55849-258-5 (cloth : alk. paper)
1. Landscape gardening. 2. Landscape architecture.
3. Landscape gardening—United States.
4. Landscape Architecture—United States.   I. Title

SB472 .S6 2000
712´.6—dc21
00-028215

British Library Cataloguing in Publication data are available.

PREFACE

The ASLA Centennial Reprint Series comprises a small library of influential historical books about American landscape architecture. The titles were selected by a committee of distinguished editors who identified them as classics, important in shaping design, planting, planning, and stewardship practices in the field and still relevant today. Each is reprinted from the original edition and introduced by a new essay that provides historical and contemporary perspective. The project commemorates the 1999 centennial of the American Society of Landscape Architects and is underwritten by the Viburnum Foundation, Rochester, New York. *Landscape-Gardening* is the second book in the series.

In his 1920 classic, O. C. Simonds makes strikingly modern reference to "open space." Although eighty years have elapsed since the publication of his book, Simonds's meaning was identical to the current one: he was describing a precious and vanishing resource. It is difficult to imagine the comparatively innocent state of the countryside that Simonds's book bemoaned as not only thoughtlessly and tastelessly compromised but endangered. What he would make of the world today is beyond imagination.

Simonds was one of the country's important early landscape architects, the progenitor of the "middle western movement" of landscape design, an influential teacher, author, founder of university programs, and the only Midwesterner among the eleven charter members of the American Society of Landscape Architects. His most important surviving works include Graceland Cemetery in Chicago, the Morton Arboretum in Lisle, Illinois, and the Nichols Arboretum, in Ann Arbor, Michigan.

Landscape-Gardening is both a fascinating historical document and an inspiring and affecting treatise on how individual citizens can become better stewards of the land. Simonds urged the study of nature as a means of developing a more refined aesthetic sense, proposing that nature can be both model and partner in design, an approach that he believed would foster better designs for parks, roadways, farms, schools, cemeteries, and suburban residences.

Simonds's book was aimed at the rural citizenry, part of a series edited by Liberty Hyde Bailey which also included *Pork Production* and *The Spraying of Plants*. These books were intended to improve agricultural practice through science, but in many cases their reach was broader. Because few books available at the time possessed the scope of Simonds's, it was also read by many landscape architects and prospective clients.

Backyard gardeners will be particularly interested in Simonds's ecological approach, which emphasized the use of existing plants and native species. "Nothing in nature is more charming than woods," he wrote. "One should have this charm in intimate relationship with one's home." Simonds's descriptions are evocative as well as pragmatic. "A lot," he suggested, "might have in one corner a thicket with red-buds at the back, then hawthorns and perhaps a black haw or an elderberry. Underneath this the leaves might be allowed to remain and protect wild flowers, like anemones, erythoniums, trilliums, and bloodroots. A thicket of this kind would, for the most part, take care of itself."

In a thoughtful introduction, Robert E. Grese, associate professor of landscape architecture and director of the Nichols Arboretum at the University of Michigan, points to the deeper purpose of Simonds's book: to inspire not only the preservation of native beauty but the restoration of degraded landscapes. We join him in the hope that this reprint will benefit the profession as it enters its second century, serving as a reminder of the foundations laid by one of its influential leaders.

To further vitalize the connections between Simonds's book and current environmental and design concerns, we have invited the Nichols Arboretum of the University of Michigan to join us as an educational partner in creating a program of lectures, tours, and associated publications to celebrate the appearance of the reprint. We are pleased to be working with them to bring the timely perspectives of O. C. Simonds to a wider audience.

Robin Karson, Executive Director
Library of American Landscape History
Amherst, Massachusetts

The Library of American Landscape History, Inc., a nonprofit organization, produces books and exhibitions about American landscape history. Its mission is to educate and thereby promote thoughtful stewardship of the land.

LIBRARY of

AMERICAN
LANDSCAPE
HISTORY

INTRODUCTION

TO THE REPRINT EDITION

ROBERT E. GRESE

America is rich in species of trees and shrubs and also in native flowers, and one who is developing an American home ought certainly to make use of the material close at hand, and thus develop a restful retreat which might with propriety be called "an American garden." . . . A retreat of this kind will give its owner and his friends endless diversion and entertainment. It will also increase his interest in all that vegetation which comes of itself along roadsides, margins of woods and streams and other out-of-the-way places. It is this awakening of our senses to the beauty that exists wherever nature is given an opportunity to show her charms that will add zest to life, give individuality to one's home, and a value to grounds far beyond that which they may have already have.   *Landscape-Gardening*, 1920

Ossian Cole Simonds (1855–1931), one of the pioneers of American landscape architecture in the late nineteenth and early twentieth centuries, is largely unknown today. Yet, at the turn of the century, he was one of the handful of individuals steadily building a tradition of American landscape design, shaping city park systems, neighborhoods, and cemeteries throughout the country. In 1920 his book *Landscape-Gardening* was published as part of Liberty Hyde Bailey's Rural Science series. Bailey, a major force in American botany and horticulture at Cornell University and a leader in the Country Life movement, sought to improve conditions in rural areas and small towns across the United States. Simonds's *Landscape-Gardening* ensured that the then-emerging field of landscape architecture would be represented in the series. Today it provides us a summary of his thinking about landscape design, conservation, and management.

When *Landscape-Gardening* was first published, it received mixed reviews. In her biography of Simonds, Barbara Geiger notes that he proudly included favorable words from several American periodicals, the London *Times,* and *The Gardener's Chronicle* as "background information about himself" to the *National Cyclopedia of Biography.*[1] However, *Landscape Architecture,* the journal of the American Society of Landscape Architects (ASLA), carried an anonymous review that criticized the book as too narrow for the scope of landscape architecture, appropriate rather as "first reading for rural clients, women's clubs, and men engaged in outdoor work in the allied professions of forestry and engineering where an appreciation of landscape beauty is much to be desired." The reviewer believed that Simonds placed far too much emphasis on scenic beauty without adequate discussion of "planning of economic uses" to be helpful to modern landscape architects.[2]

For Simonds, however, landscape design had a much broader scope, grounded in nature, which was both partner and model. Simonds was one of the pioneers of a movement to develop ecological practices in landscape design.[3] Throughout the book, the reader is always encouraged to learn to read the landscape and respect its subtle beauty. Much as Liberty Hyde Bailey had done in *The Holy Earth* (1916) and as Aldo Leopold would do later in *A Sand County Almanac* (1949), Simonds here promotes an ethical attitude toward the land, suggesting an approach to design heavily intertwined with stewardship responsibilities and civic pride. For Simonds, this was clearly a personal mission, born from a sense of loss. He was seeing places that he had learned to treasure as a child abruptly changed and developed, and he feared a generation that was becoming complacent in their acceptance of a dull sameness in the landscape. Through *Landscape-Gardening,* he hoped to awaken people to the natural beauty around them and help them see how

O. C. Simonds. Date unknown. *Courtesy Simonds family.*

this beauty could be incorporated into daily landscapes through careful planning and design.

The challenge today is the same that Simonds and his contemporaries faced: to convince the public that nature can be adapted and used as a model for our designed landscapes. For Simonds, gardening involved not just the backyard but the larger landscape as well. He was among the earliest designers to champion intercon-

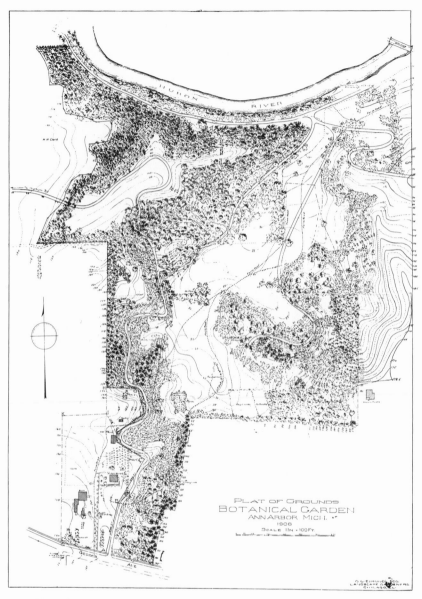

"Plat of Grounds, Botanical Garden [now Nichols Arboretum], Ann Arbor." 1906. *Courtesy Graduate Library, University of Michigan, Ann Arbor.*

A view in the Nichols Arboretum, 1998. *Photo by Carol Betsch.*

nected park and boulevard systems (today known as greenways), particularly along rivers and other water courses. Cities where he
worked—Ann Arbor, Michigan, Quincy, Illinois, and Madison,
Wisconsin—benefited from his foresight in protecting valuable
natural settings as the city grew around them. For many readers,

Simonds's writing will recall the messages conveyed by the better-known individuals he saw as his mentors—Humphry Repton, Andrew Jackson Downing, and Frederick Law Olmsted Sr.[4] His aim, as he notes in his introductory chapter, was to nurture an appreciation for natural beauty, to stimulate a desire to make the country more beautiful through landscape gardening.

Simonds's fascination with nature began early on his family's farm near Grand Rapids, Michigan. As a child, he learned to identify the flowers, shrubs, and trees on the farm and in the surrounding countryside.[5] One of Simonds's favorite stories was of a man who taught him to appreciate the beauty of simple scenes along the roadside.

> When I was about seven or eight . . . my job was to deliver milk from my father's farm to a customer a mile away. For this, I had to get up at five in the morning and walk along a hillside road. I didn't like getting up so early and I didn't like the long walk; and as I walked along, I felt sorry for myself. My mind kept gloomily on the fate that made me take such early walks. Then, one day I met a remarkable man. I hadn't seen him before, nor have I seen him since, yet that meeting changed my life. He stopped to talk to me; and I suppose I complained about my long walks in the early morning, because he very kindly said, "My friend, how mistaken you are! What a pleasure in life you are missing. Instead of complaining and thinking gloomy thoughts, you should realize what a joy it is to be able to walk along this hillside and to observe the growth and change of the trees. Do you see the mist rising over the valley, creeping upward among the alder branches? Do you see the first rays of the sun in the tree tops on the maples heralding the sun before you actually see it? What a privilege you have, my friend, to be able to take this walk every day. I feel lucky if I can get here at this hour once a month. Do you know the aspens and the red-barked dogwoods? Count them as you walk along and you will find you will end your walk all too soon."[6]

It was a transformative experience. At an uncommonly early age Simonds learned to appreciate nature's simpler pleasures and laid the groundwork for a life of helping others do the same. The chief

aim of landscape gardening, in his mind, was to build this appreciation of the commonplace and to stimulate a desire to protect the
beauty of natural places. The later sale and development of the farm
deeply saddened him and, in part, led to his strongly held belief in
land conservation.

As a young man Simonds studied civil engineering at the University of Michigan in Ann Arbor, graduating in 1878. During his
last two years of college, he attended lectures by William La Baron
Jenney, a professor of architecture and engineering at the time, who
was known for his work in developing the modern skyscraper as
well as designs for Chicago's West Parks.[7] Jenney apparently per-
suaded young Simonds to take up architecture together with civil
engineering, and on graduating, Simonds joined Jenney's office
in Chicago. His first project there involved running a survey of
Graceland Cemetery.

In 1880, Simonds and William Holabird, one of his architectural
colleagues, teamed up to form their own firm, Holabird & Simonds.
Initially, their sole client was Graceland, where Simonds in particular became completely engrossed in developing the landscape and
in 1881 was named superintendent. Part of the firm's work involved
preparing designs for an office and railroad station at the cemetery,
projects that required additional architectural expertise, so they hired
Martin Roche, who had worked with them in Jenney's office. The
enterprise of Holabird, Simonds & Roche was short-lived, however, as Simonds resigned in 1883 to devote his full energies to
his expanding responsibilities at Graceland.[8] As superintendent,
Simonds continued developing a large addition that he had begun
while still in Jenney's employ. The work included "putting in drains,
excavating a lake [Willowmere], grading and building roads, and grading the various sections."[9] Through these improvements, Simonds
was striving to make Graceland a model "park" cemetery.

While implementing the changes, Simonds came to know Bryan
Lathrop, president of the Graceland Cemetery Association and one

University of Michigan central campus at the time Simonds attended. *Courtesy Simonds family.*

Students on the central campus. *Courtesy Simonds family.*

O. C. Simonds. Date unknown; likely about the time he began working on Graceland Cemetery, Chicago. *Courtesy Simonds family.*

of Chicago's leading citizens, active in a wide variety of civic affairs and fervent champion of landscape gardening. Lathrop soon became a mentor to Simonds. He took the young man to Cincinnati to meet Adolph Strauch and study Strauch's work at Spring Grove, one of the country's most beautiful park cemeteries. He also shared his own library with him. The texts Simonds found there—works by Loudon, Repton, Downing, and others—he later credited as in-

Buena Avenue entrance to Graceland Cemetery.

Planting of hawthorn along drive at Graceland.

Both photos courtesy Landscape Architecture Concentration, School of Natural Resources and Environment, University of Michigan, Ann Arbor.

spiring many of his own ideas. Simonds considered Lathrop's judgment on a par with "that of Repton, Robinson, Downing, Olmsted, Cleveland, or Strauch" and included two essays by him as an appendix to *Landscape-Gardening*.[10] For the young Simonds, the years at Graceland with Lathrop provided an ideal opportunity to hone his skills as a landscape gardener and experiment with new ideas in design. He drew heavily from his knowledge of the common plants of the midwestern countryside as he worked to make the cemetery "a place of quiet retreat, a place of beauty, a place of park like character" as well as a refuge for birds in the heart of the city.[11]

Graceland was widely celebrated—receiving a silver medal at the Paris Exposition in 1900—and frequently featured in the early professional publications, and his work there firmly established Simonds's reputation as a talented and sensitive designer. During this time he had also begun to build a private practice, and through his growing reputation and with the help of Lathrop and other influential friends, Simonds secured a variety of commissions. These ranged from residential properties in the city to large country estates, city parks and park systems for towns throughout the Midwest, portions of several major college campuses, subdivision designs, golf courses, and arboretums. By the time of his death in 1931, Simonds was said to have practiced in every state of the union, and in his obituaries he was named the "dean" of landscape architecture.

Simonds's work in Chicago occurred at a pivotal moment in the history of the profession. He was a transitional figure between the early designers such as Olmsted and Jenney and the second generation of practitioners such as Jens Jensen, who began his career somewhat later than Simonds and with whom he has often been associated as a founder of a unique "prairie style" of landscape design. Simonds also forged important connections with many of the professionals who were defining the early literature—Warren H. Manning, Wilhelm Miller, and Liberty Hyde Bailey.

At the time that Simonds wrote *Landscape-Gardening*, he and others were in the process of defining the role of a young profession (variously known as landscape architecture, landscape design, or, simply, landscape gardening—the term Simonds preferred)[12] in a range of design work, from residential grounds to city parks, college campuses to regional planning. The ASLA, founded in 1899, sought to achieve professional status for practicing landscape architects. For Simonds and his contemporaries, however, landscape architecture was not a narrowly defined field but rather one that necessarily intersected and merged with engineering, architecture, art, music, ecology, city planning, and forestry, among others. Like many of his generation, Simonds had received no formal training in landscape architecture—training was done in related fields such as architecture, civil engineering, and horticulture—and he learned landscape design through intensive lifelong study, much of it on his own. His teachers included informal mentors such as Bryan Lathrop, who readily shared books and other resources, and elder practitioners such as Strauch, William Robinson, Olmsted, and H. W. S. Cleveland. Clearly, he also learned from his association with contemporaries such as Jensen, Manning, and others who served with him on various boards and later in the ASLA.

Simonds himself took a lead in furthering formal education in the profession, working to develop landscape design programs at the universities where he was hired to prepare site plans (Iowa State, Michigan State, and University of Chicago). It was at his alma mater, however, where he was finally successful, in 1909.[13] Simonds maintained strong ties to University of Michigan program, supplying most of its teachers from his office in Chicago and commuting to Ann Arbor regularly to give lectures himself (which later became the basis of *Landscape-Gardening*). The range of his lecture topics—and the book—provides a model for the breadth of scope necessary for today's landscape architects, who also must practice in a truly interdisciplinary mode.[14] Broad training, Simonds believed, especially that which cultivated an appreciation for beauty, benefited everyone.[15]

The Simonds family home at 929 Montrose Avenue, Chicago, showing Simonds's observation platform. *Courtesy Simonds family.*

Simonds took a leadership role as well in each of the several professions in which he had received training. He was a co-founder and president of the Association of American Cemetery Superintendents and was considered the nation's leading expert in "rural" cemetery design. One of the founding members of the American Park and Outdoor Art Association (organized 1897), he served as chair of the committee devoted to rural planning. Simonds also was the only Midwesterner to be counted among the founders of the ASLA, and in 1913 became the first non-Easterner to be elected its president. He also maintained an active role in the Western Society of Engineers from 1886 until his death in 1931.

Simonds was a figure, too, in the celebrated Chicago renaissance, a period just before World War I when a group of talented artists, writers, designers, social reformers, business leaders, and politicians focused their energies on making their city the center of the midwestern United States and a cultural center second to none. Like Jensen and many of the other leading architects and planners there, Simonds was an active member of the University Club, the City Club, and the Cliff Dwellers. He served on the Special Park Commission formed in 1899 to develop long-range plans for the Chicago parks and from 1903 to 1913 and 1917 to 1921 designed extensions of Lincoln Park from Diversey Parkway north to Devon Avenue.

Simonds always maintained his youthful fascination with nature in all its forms. His son Herbert described a small covered platform that Simonds had built on the roof of his house from which he could watch lightning storms over the city and Lake Michigan.[16] Farming and forestry practices were a lifelong interest. Both Simonds and his wife, Martha, belonged to a close-knit group of six couples which they called the "Ravenswood Home College," who met for discussions on scientific and other topics. And the family planted large vegetable gardens both at their home in Chicago and across Lake Michigan at their summer property.[17]

For Simonds, this summer property and the small community of people that developed around it held a very special meaning. While at the University of Michigan, Simonds had developed a close friendship with another engineering student, John Butler Johnson (later dean of the College of Engineering at the University of Wisconsin). The two secured a government contract to prepare a geodetic survey of a section of the eastern shore of Lake Michigan in the vicinity of Saugatuck, where much of the area had been cut over to provide timber to help rebuild Chicago after the Great Fire of 1871. Simonds and Johnson became fascinated with a deserted mill and the mile-long ravine and land surrounding it, and promised each other to buy a few acres when they could scrape together the money. Simonds began acquiring property along the ravine in 1889; Johnson finally bought about an acre of the lakeshore in 1897. Over the years, Simonds added to his acreage and used the land to experiment with

The old mill and mill pond in Simonds's ravine at Pier Cove. *Courtesy Simonds family.*

The Orchard House at Pier Cove, Michigan, shortly after Simonds bought the property in 1889. *Courtesy Simonds family.*

Gathering on the beach at Pier Cove. *Courtesy Simonds family.*

Celebration at Pier Cove (Simonds in hat in back row). *Courtesy Simonds family.*

Canoeing on the creek at Pier Cove. *Courtesy Simonds family.*

a variety of plantings and reforestation efforts. Simonds remodeled an old house on the property, which became the family's summer retreat. The Simondses and Johnsons, together with a few other families, formed a small summer community known as The Cove.[18]

Reminiscences of people who grew up knowing him at The Cove provide a vivid portrait of Simonds. Punctual, not particularly outgoing, and with little use for idle talk, he was an avid reader who also enjoyed taking long walks, particularly through the ravine. At the same time, he showed great fondness for the children and attempted to share with them his love of plants and other natural features. He regarded many of the plants as friends and would describe their characteristics in great detail to anyone who came along with him on his walks. He also had a small canoe and took children on excursions with him around the old mill pond and up the creek that ran through the ravine. He is described as having an almost missionary zeal to inspire his love of nature in those around him.[19]

Simonds's passion for sharing nature with children was expressed in other ways as well. For example, at the founding meeting of the Illinois Out-Door Improvement Association in 1909, he proposed three resolutions for nature education in the state which were adopted by the organization:

> 1—That the children be given more instruction in outdoor art and taught to appreciate natural beauty,
> 2—That this instruction should be given in an incidental way and not as an additional course which would add to the burdens of the pupil,
> 3—That as a preparation for giving such instruction, special courses should be given in our normal schools and higher institutions of learning.[20]

Simonds's reclamation of the cut-over ravine was a personal expression of the same impulse that led to his professional efforts to replant and reforest degraded landscapes: he believed deeply in the aesthetic value of wooded areas. In a 1907 report issued by the Michigan Forestry Commission, Simonds describes the beauty of the state's woodlands and urges their preservation for their aesthetic as well as economic and functional benefits. He points to the impact such wild lands had on his own youth and presents a hope for the next generation: "It seems to me that I could have no better wish for the children of the future than that they should enjoy native woods, with the wild flowers that go with them, as much as I enjoyed, many years ago, the unbroken forest near Grand Rapids."[21] This idea became a major theme of *Landscape-Gardening*.

Simonds's work has often been linked with that of Jens Jensen, and the two men's careers were parallel in many ways. Both Simonds and Jensen emphasized elements of the native midwestern landscape in their work, and both have been identified as leading forces behind a distinctive "prairie" style.[22] In a letter to Wilhelm Miller, who had worked as an editor for Liberty Hyde Bailey, Simonds clearly expressed an appreciation of Jensen's work. According to Alfred Caldwell, who had worked closely with Jensen, Simonds was one of the few landscape architects whose work Jensen admired. Marshall Johnson, Jensen's son-in-law and chief draftsman, noted that Simonds would occasionally drop by the Jensen studio in Ravinia on Chicago's North Shore for a visit.[23] Both Simonds and Jensen belonged to many of the same organizations, served on the same boards, and spoke at the same conferences. Still, there are few clues as to how they related personally. Jensen was a fiery, tempestuous individual; Simonds, quiet and reserved.[24] There were differences in design philosophy as well. At a meeting of the ASLA in Chicago in 1926, Simonds was asked to respond to Jensen's talk in which Jensen had stated his adamant belief that "native plants and the 'native styles' are particularly suitable for the home garden" and "voiced his disapproval of the formal garden as an importation understood only by a few, and inappropriate to the manner of life of our people." Put on the spot, Simonds, who was less dogmatic in his approach, diplomatically noted that designs "need not always be informal in the vicinity of the house," and should attend as well to concerns of "comfort, convenience, and enjoyment, and attractive planting."[25] Clearly he did not want to offend Jensen, whose work he respected, but he did want to express views consistent with his own principles. Although both Simonds and Jensen were passionately devoted to conservation efforts, there is no evidence that Simonds belonged to either of Jensen's conservation groups, the Prairie Club or the Friends of Our Native Landscape. Simonds's daughter Gertrude, however, was quite active in the Prairie Club and helped lead occasional outings in addition to serving on its board of directors.[26]

Simonds also shared deep philosophical beliefs with Warren Manning, another conservation-minded landscape architect. Manning's account of a meeting of the American Civic Association in 1929 in Illinois provides insight into Simonds's role in the organization and his involvement with Manning.[27] The meeting included a rail tour between Springfield and Chicago. Along the way, Manning recorded, "the prairie values were expressed by Mr. O. C. Simonds of Chicago as we passed over them on the way to Monticello." Simonds (who had an excellent voice) broke into song:

> A pleasant mansion in the west on prairie lands for me
> Now smooth as billows all abreast, now rolling as the sea
> There blooms the flowers in splendor bright
> There shine the stars with glorious light
> Serene upon the prairie lea, the prairie lea.

During the trip, which included stops in Urbana, Bloomington, El Paso, and Joliet, the group discussed issues of conservation and planning. Manning reported their talk of "the importance of comprehensive planning to anticipate the future growth needs of the state, its regions and towns, and the need of conserving and developing the beauty factors as well as the utilitarian needs and also the importance of preserving the individuality of cities in their development, as well as of regions." (In this, Manning was articulating the regional planning themes he had explored in his National Plan Study Brief as well as in his journal *Billerica*, to which Simonds had contributed.)[28] He closes his narrative of the meeting by drawing "attention to the good work that is being done in Illinois by the Friends of Our Native Landscape in laying down 'A Park and Forest Policy for Illinois.'" Whether Jensen was along on the tour is unclear, but Manning obviously was aware of Jensen's conservation work. The purpose of the *Park and Forest Policy*, written at least partly by Jensen, was "to cultivate in every individual a more active pleasure in the world of the open. To save all places of beauty and interest that will tie the present and future generations of America to the past, and serve as playgrounds for the people and sanctuaries for wild plant and animal life."[29] Whatever their personal relationship, Manning, Simonds, and Jensen were connected by strong ideological as well as professional ties.

Most of the books in the Rural Science series focus on farming and country life, but *Landscape-Gardening* reflects Bailey's interest in

home landscaping and gardening. When he first was putting together the series, Bailey wanted to include a volume on landscape
art. In 1896 he wrote to Manning asking him to prepare a "planting
manual" useful to homeowners.[30] Manning was likely in the process
of writing *A Handbook for Planning and Planting Small Home Grounds*
for the Stout Manual Training School in Menomonie, Wisconsin,
which was published in 1899. Although a book by him never mate-
rialized as part of the series, Manning did write several articles on
home landscape design for Bailey's *Country Life in America* and contribute an essay on "the art of designing landscapes" in the "Landscape Gardening" section of Bailey's 1916 edition of the *Standard
Cyclopedia of Horticulture*.[31] For whatever reason, Bailey then turned
to Simonds.

It was a natural choice. Simonds had earlier written several important essays for Bailey, most notably "Landscape cemeteries" and
"Shrubbery" in the 1916 *Standard Cyclopedia,* as well as occasional
pieces for other of Bailey's publications.[32] Wilhelm Miller, as Bailey's
assistant and editor of *Country Life in America,* frequently featured
Simond's work in the magazine. Bailey must have regarded Simonds
as something of a kindred spirit. Both men had grown up on farms
in western Michigan, where they had first learned to love nature.
Bailey's primary training and work had centered on botany and horticulture, but he had become interested in environmental and agricultural extension education, philosophy, teaching, writing, and ed-
iting. He wrote extensively on home gardening and landscaping and
included a program in landscape art in the curriculum of the Cornell
College of Agriculture during his tenure there as dean. About the
same time, Simonds was helping to establish the similar program at
Michigan.

Simonds's emphasis on the study of nature as a critical component of landscape design training would have appealed to Bailey,
who helped found the Nature Study movement of the early twentieth century. Bailey, like Simonds, believed that people should ap-

proach nature with a strong sense of environmental stewardship and humility—nature was the "teacher"[33]—and he was committed to making botanical, agricultural, and horticultural information easily available to the general public. The Rural Science series exemplified the best of these efforts. The series can also be seen as an outgrowth of Bailey's involvement with Theodore Roosevelt's presidential Commission on Country Life, which had been formed in 1909. The commission resulted in the establishment, among other improvements, of a nationwide federal extension service and agricultural education in public high schools. Bailey would have especially appreciated Simonds's broad view of landscape gardening in relation to improving the quality of life for both urban and rural people, promoting conservation values, and extending principles of land stewardship in all aspects of planning. These major themes run through various chapters of *Landscape-Gardening*.

"The purpose of this book," Simonds states at the outset, "is to help make our country more beautiful." Beauty is intrinsically linked to our individual and collective happiness. The aim of landscape gardening, "the youngest of the arts," is to "improve and organize the landscape" based on careful study of patterns seen in nature. Simonds had a broad vision of landscape gardening as helping to inspire the protection and creation of beautiful and functional landscapes, something that should be done on a comprehensive scale. Its practice had applications ranging from wild landscapes to rural farms to suburban areas to cities. Indeed, the study of landscape gardening was not only important to those interested in professional practice but of potential and far-reaching interest to everyone: "a knowledge of this subject, even though rudimentary will add much to the joy of living. . . . a study of landscape gardening, even though not followed by a professional career in landscape work, will, I am sure, cause one to see and enjoy many things which he would otherwise miss; to think more of his country; to establish a better home, and lead a more useful and happy existence."[34]

Early view of Morton Arboretum main road, planned to pass under arching oak limb. *Courtesy Morton Arboretum, Lisle, Ill.*

In this belief of a larger necessity for landscape gardening, Simonds recalls those earlier practitioners he deeply admired— Humphry Repton, Andrew Jackson Downing, William Robinson, Frederick Law Olmsted Sr., and Adolph Strauch. He also echoes the sentiments of Bryan Lathrop, to whom he dedicated the book, and Liberty Hyde Bailey. Simonds quoted Bailey in his introductory lecture at Michigan: "This great new profession is to have much influence on the development of life and thought. It is to relate our surroundings to the increasing artistic temper of our lives. It must choose and preserve and improve the best landscapes, and make them accessible, without rendering them artificial and hateful."

The aspect of chapter 1, "The Aims of Landscape-Gardening," perhaps most useful to today's reader is Simonds's discussion of the general principles germane to the practice. The landscape gardener, like the landscape painter, must study nature, observing "the sky lines, the masses of foliage, the lights and shadows, the varying colors and shapes of leaves and flowers, the lay of the land, the reflections in water." The work of a landscape gardener is guided by certain rules, including the striving for unity (achieved, for example, by the repetition of dominant characteristics), attention to multiple points from which to view the landscape, and preserving or creating a sense of harmony and balance, contrast and variety "to make a scene restful." Simonds also articulates an approach to composition in which the focus of interest is deliberately placed off-center to increase a sense of mystery and entice the viewer to investigate the landscape further.[35] In explaining this approach, he describes features that are actually common in his own work: "woods into which one gets glimpses leading to unknown depths, bays of lakes disappearing behind islands or promontories, lawns partly hidden by projecting groups of shrubs." Simonds frequently created irregular boundaries of shrubs and trees around open meadow spaces and water surfaces deliberately to hide some parts of the landscape from immediate view, the effect of which was to make the property appear much larger and to invite the viewer to move through the landscape. Miller featured one such of Simonds's designs in his 1914 *Country Life* article "A Series of Outdoor Salons."[36]

Few of Simonds's drawings have survived, but his 1907 design plan for the Julia Larned estate at Hubbard Woods, Illinois, is extant and provides a useful case study of how he applied the principles described in *Landscape-Gardening*.[37] Here, Simonds massed trees, shrubs, and flowers carefully to shape a series of spaces that flowed from one to the next through "doorways" of shrubs and trees. A generous terrace wraps around the southwest corner of the house, and Simonds framed a series of views from it with large trees near the edge. At the end of these views are masses of wildflowers, including goldenrod species that would have been particularly brilliant in late summer and fall. Around the borders of the property are dense plantings of trees and shrubs that provide privacy—wild

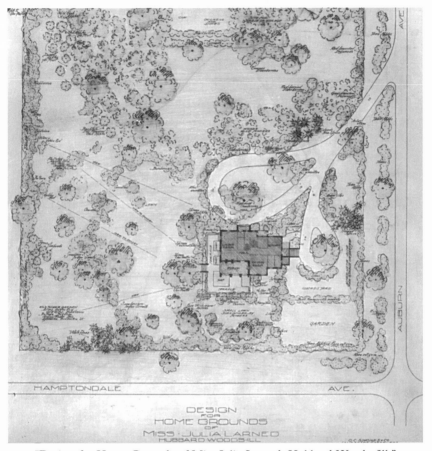

"Design for Home Grounds of Miss Julia Larned, Hubbard Woods, Ill."
1907. *Courtesy Landscape Architecture Concentration, School of Natural Resources and Environment, University of Michigan, Ann Arbor.*

crab apples, "thorn apples" (hawthorn), prairie rose (*Rosa setigera*), "gray-branched" and "red-branched" dogwoods, white pines, and prickly ash. Around the house he planted horticultural species such as forsythia, lilac, myrtle (periwinkle) and bulbs, *Spiraea rotundifolia* and *van houteii*, and *Rosa wichuriana*. Farther away, however, native species were used for the most part, such as elderberries, snowberry and Indian current, *Ceanothus,* and wildflowers (including asters, goldenrods, lilies, *Eupatorium, Boltonia, Lysimachia, Rudbeckia,* cardinal flower, and iris). At the north edge of the property are utilitarian areas for cows, chickens, and doves, a site for a "stable or garage," a path to a "cow pasture," and a cluster of dwarf apple trees.

Although Simonds does not directly address the interdisciplinary aspects of landscape design as we see it today, he does note its synthetic quality, suggesting that it joins "the work of the architect or engineer with that of nature." He points to the designer's need for skills often associated with related disciplines. Landscape gardening, like architecture, must address issues of "comfort, safety, and use." Like sculptors, landscape gardeners are concerned with the forms and quality of surfaces. Like those in the natural sciences, landscape gardeners must have an understanding of geology, botany, and chemistry. But unlike the others, landscape gardeners have to deal with issues of time: the landscape gardener must be "a dreamer more than most designers because it may take years for his designs to develop."

In the next two chapters, Simonds establishes a background of conservation and natural resources against which to read the ideas about design and landscape gardening discussed in the rest of the book. In chapter 2, "The Saving of Natural Features and Resources," Simonds reiterates his call for the consideration of the beauty and recreational value and not just utilitarian value of natural resources, which he had earlier urged in the Michigan Forestry Commission report. This was a relatively new concept at the time, particularly with regard to forest resources. In the 1860s, George Perkins Marsh had argued for their conservation primarily to protect timber and water supplies and to prevent soil erosion.[38] Forty years later, Gifford Pinchot, the first chief of the U.S. Forest Service, echoed these concerns when he called for the application of scientific principles to the management of national forest and water resources.[39] In the

1890s, however, Charles Eliot argued for the museum value of forest lands around Boston and urged their protection as part of a system of metropolitan "reservations."[40] Similarly, during the teens, Professor Frank A. Waugh of the Massachusetts Agricultural College conducted extensive studies with the Forest Service and urged that the aesthetic and recreational value of forest lands be considered in addition to their timber value. Waugh's booklets, *Recreation Uses on the National Forests* and *Landscape Engineering in the National Forests*, provided some of the first concise arguments for comprehensive recreational planning in the National Forests and had a significant impact on both National Forest and National Park properties throughout the United States.[41] Warren Manning had also echoed these themes in his planning studies published in *Billerica* and the National Plan.

In chapter 3, "Land," Simonds foreshadows the modern view that soil and geological resources are important to landscape design. He points to the need for understanding geology, physiography, and soil characteristics such as its chemistry, biota, and aeration as background for any landscape design effort. These ideas parallel today's thinking regarding landscape ecosystem classification, which uses landscape physiography as a basis for mapping landscape patterns.[42] Charles Eliot had championed a similar process of landscape analysis in his work for the Metropolitan Reservations in Boston, and he in turn influenced Warren Manning, who at the time worked with Eliot in the Olmsted office and organized much of the fieldwork to carry out a land inventory for the Metropolitan Park Commission.[43] As a member (with Jensen) of Chicago's Special Park Commission, Simonds had helped develop a similar inventory of the Chicago area from 1899 to 1903, using soils, geologic features, and vegetation patterns to identify priority lands for protection as regional forest preserves and parks.

The next three chapters present Simonds's ideas on planting design. He points to the wide variety of material available to the landscape gardener, including not only the more typical trees, shrubs, vines, herbaceous flowering plants, and ferns, but also mosses, lichens, and fungi.[44] (Little detail on specific choices is given, however, since Simonds intended that readers consult other sources for plants appropriate to their own regions.) Given Simonds's commitment to protection and conservation of natural resources, his remark that "new beauty is discovered in well-known plants," especially familiar native species, is not surprising. "Sumacs, elderberries, hazel bushes, goldenrods and asters," he writes, "once considered so common as to command little more respect than weeds, are found to be really valuable in landscape-making." At Graceland Cemetery and in the various parks and gardens Simonds created throughout the country, he emphasized locally native species.

Wilhelm Miller applauded this approach in *The Illinois Way of Beautifying the Farm* (1914) and *The Prairie Spirit in Landscape Gardening* (1915), and attributed the origin of a "middle-western movement" in landscape gardening to Simonds: "In 1880 Mr. Simonds began to transplant from the wilds the common Illinois species of oak, maple, ash, hornbeam, pepperidge, thorn apple, witch hazel, panicled dogwood, sheepberry, elder, and the like. . . . The guiding spirit was that respect for the quieter beauties of native vegetation which comes to every cultured person after he has lived a few years among the showiest plants from all foreign lands as assembled in ordinary nurseries and in the front yards of beginners. Graceland was to be a place of rest and peace, not a museum or gaudy show. Should not the same ideal prevail in our home grounds?"[45]

Miller characterized Simonds's work (together with Jensen's and Walter Burley Griffin's) as defining a new "prairie style" of landscape design, much like the "prairie style" of architecture. In his view, the crux of the prairie spirit was the use of local native plants, and in his writings, Miller proselytized this approach with an almost religious zeal and patriotic fervor.[46] Simonds, however, was not convinced that his work constituted a prairie style—or any style

A typical Simonds planting using native species—cow parsnips—in the Nichols Arboretum, 1998. *Photo by Carol Betsch.*

for that matter. As he wrote to Miller, "I do not yet feel that there is a distinct 'Prairie Style.' A great deal is said about the formal or artificial style and a natural or informal style. I regret this and pay no attention to any so-called style in my work or designing. I simply do that which, to my mind, will make the most beautiful effect."[47] In fact, Simonds was not a purist about using native plants and occasionally used such naturalized species such as Hall's hon-

Simonds's planting using two hawthorns as a "gateway" to outdoor rooms. From Wilhelm Miller, "A Series of Outdoor Salons," *Country Life in America,* April 1914.

eysuckle (*Lonicera japonica*), now, ironically, considered a rampant ecological pest. Many of his planting plans also included similarly dangerous horticultural introductions such as the shrub honeysuckles (*Lonicera morrowi* and *tatarica*), common buckthorn (*Rhamnus cathartica*), and Norway maple (*Acer platanoides*)—species banned in some communities today because of the harm they cause to nearby natural areas. (In Simonds's defense, it should be said that only in the past twenty-five years or so have the damages wrought by "escapees" from horticultural plantings been noted within the scientific, conservation, and design communities.)[48]

Simonds continues the discussion of his planting philosophy in chapters 5 and 6. The arrangement of plantings, he suggests, is often more important than actual plant selection; the forms of plants

Lake Willowmere, Graceland Cemetery. *Courtesy Landscape Architecture Concentration, School of Natural Resources and Environment, University of Michigan, Ann Arbor.*

should highlight particular features of the design. For example, broad trees and shrubs should be planted on the projections of foliage masses, whereas narrow, upright plants should be placed in the bays. (This strategy was also employed by Jensen, and Miller believed it to be one of the distinguishing features of the prairie style, echoing the horizontal lines of the flat prairie landscape.) Simonds also stresses the importance of following nature's patterns in planting but warns that achieving "natural" effects can be quite a challenge: artful management is necessary to maintain an attractive arrangement and well-framed views. The practical information contained in chapter 6 is as up-to-date today as when it was first written and demonstrates Simonds's thorough understanding of plants and planting for long-term effects in the landscape.

Simonds was equally sensitive to wetland and aquatic habitats, and knowledgeable about their role in nature and the landscape. Among the most celebrated features of Graceland Cemetery are the two ponds known as Willowmere and Hazelmere. These artificial bodies of water were carefully fitted into the topography to appear natural, and their shorelines were gracefully planted with dense vegetation; their mirrorlike surfaces reflect the surrounding landscape as well as the sky. In "Water," Simonds instructs the reader on how to create such artificial ponds, but the bulk of the chapter is devoted to naturally occurring wetlands and aquatic habitats. Critical of the common practice of using wetlands as dumping grounds, Simonds urges their protection and incorporation into both local designs and larger planning efforts. His ideas are as relevant today, when despite our increased appreciation of their beauty and understanding of their critical ecological value, recently protected wetlands are still regarded by many people only as stumbling blocks to development.

Simonds had considerable expertise in residential design and was eager to share his practical experience. His focus in "Home Grounds" is on serving people's needs and creating functional, attractive home settings. His unpretentious approach emphasizes comfort, not perceived notions of "taste." The design of the front yard, for example, is discussed entirely from the perspective from the house, from porches, or from the yard itself—almost no attention is given to the view from the street. In fact, Simonds suggests that to create a feeling of privacy and "repose," the public street should be "excluded from view," offering only "glimpses" of the yard to passersby. This idea ran counter to the trend at the time and even today, when open front lawns with a limited skirt of shrubs at the foundation of the house are still the norm, and the view from the street is the overriding concern.

Simonds's sensitivity to the subtleties of design is apparent throughout the "Home Grounds" chapter. In the layout of walks and drives, he pays attention to how people move through and experience the landscape. He advocates open space "to show sky, clouds and sunshine" with careful consideration to the graceful outlines of the trees, shrubs, and other plantings and to preserving and enhancing distant views where they exist. He also encourages the use of plantings that bring out the best of each season. Rather than relying as usual on evergreen plants "to provide winter color," he appreciates the winter effect of deciduous plants which "may be exceedingly interesting, due to the various shades of color shown by the bark of twigs and trunks of trees, to the forms and colors of buds, and to the method of branching."

Homeowners, Simonds believes, have a lot of freedom in selecting the design style that allows them to accentuate particular features of their property. Having said as much, however, he goes on to dispatch several possibilities. There is, for instance, "the impossibility of raising cypresses and other plants found in the formal gardens of Italy, or even plants resembling them." Formal flower gardens hold little interest for him—he even suggests that cultivated flowers be grouped in a garden in "a less commanding position" and associated with the vegetable garden. (For readers who do want to consider a flower garden, he notes that there are many books available on the subject.) "Colonial gardens" might be considered suitable because "the climate and soil in this country are substantially the same that they were one or two hundred years ago," and "there is a fascination in the flowers that our grandmothers raised, aside from their intrinsic beauty." But, Simonds suggests, a native garden might be even more appropriate, and although he does not directly advocate it, clearly his predilection is for such an approach. "Now that the woods have largely disappeared from those regions where there is most home building," he remarks, "the native growth is more appreciated." He elaborates: "The fear that some persons have of bringing natural beauty, that is, the beauty of untrimmed trees and bushes, of natural slopes, ravines, streams, and lakes, near a house, would seem to be groundless, since there can be no more objection to hav-

Simonds's sketch of a small garden room. *Courtesy Bentley Historical Library, University of Michigan, Ann Arbor.*

ing a window-frame enclose a beautiful picture which the objects named would make, than there is to having a similar picture hung on the wall of a room." On smaller lots, he suggests, homeowners might have "thickets" of native plants. Once again he reprises the theme: landscape design can be a means of cultivating a broader appreciation of nature.

In the remaining chapters of the book, Simonds covers various aspects of the broader reaches of landscape gardening. In chapter 9, he returns to the place of his own formative experience—the farm. Worthy of the same careful treatment as home grounds in general, farmsteads can be designed according to the same principles. He urges farmers to preserve qualities of nature on their property, for one of the true advantages of farm life is a relationship to nature. While "other men and women work in their offices, their shops, their factories and their kitchens all their lives" and dream of retiring to a more natural setting, "the farmer can spend not only his declining years but his entire life in enjoying nature." Echoing the words of the stranger he had met along the milk route as a boy, he writes of the farmer: "When he sees the beauty of nature; when he realizes the comfort that he enjoys, the satisfaction of breathing pure air, of having freedom beyond that of most men, the pleasure of listening to the songs of birds, looking at the expanse of sky, the beauty of woodlands, of sunrises and sunsets . . . his declining years may be postponed far beyond those of the average man."

In "Landscape-Gardening for Arid and Semi-Arid Regions," Simonds turns to a discussion of regionally appropriate landscape design. In the American Southwest, particularly New Mexico and Arizona, for example, too much of landscape design has consisted in simply transporting ideas about gardens from the humid eastern half of the country. Instead, landscape gardeners in this region should emphasize the beautiful rocks and views, use vegetation more sparsely, and pay careful attention to breezes and elevation differences. (An instance of Simonds's occasional self-contradiction can be found here. He writes that "it is unwise to attempt to change Colorado or Arizona to give them the appearance of Ohio or Georgia"; then, in the next sentence, he mentions visiting western towns that were "entirely destitute of trees and seemed . . . most forlorn and ugly in appearance" but were "improved" after residents planted "shade trees, bushes and flowers.")[49]

Simonds's training as a civil engineer and his study of landscape features inform his approach to the design of "Public Thoroughfares" and "Grounds of Railway Stations and Rights of Way," which he considers opportunities for enhancing the beauty of both countryside and city. He pleads for fitting transportation routes carefully into existing topography and preserving native vegetation along their edges, describing the beauty along a prairie road—one of the four types he discusses—which combined views of cultural features (farm fields, orchards, and farm complexes) with a matrix of native prairie flora and occasional clumps of bur oak or cottonwood. Similarly, along railroad rights of way, protection of native flora would enhance rail travel. During Simonds's time and before the use of herbicides, many of our roadsides provided such a refuge for native flora.[50]

Simonds continues this larger scope in chapter 13, where he presents his ideas on parks and park systems. He echoes the egalitarian ideas of Frederick Law Olmsted Sr. in his definition of the purpose of the city park: "to preserve, restore, develop, and make accessible natural scenery" for people who are unable to escape the "brick walls, paved streets, and the noises of a city," so that they might recuperate in nature. "A park," he states, "is not primarily a place for play, but rather to feed one's soul." The major problem facing park commissions, however, is the conflict of interests surrounding the purpose of a park—then, as now, everyone believed that a park was meant for their particular hobby or sport. Simonds was involved in several park systems throughout the Midwest, including the Madison Park and Pleasure Drive Association in Madison, Wisconsin, various parks in Quincy, Springfield, and Dixon, Illinois, and, in

Michigan, the Grand Rapids Park and Boulevard Association and the Ann Arbor system.[51] His ideas reflect the prevailing notion of the time, that networks of parks in a range of scale should be developed, from city squares and triangles to township, county, state, and national parks and forest preserves. He put this idea to work in Chicago, when he and the other Special Park Commissioners divided the city into a series of zones, recommending the creation of small parks and playgrounds in the most populous areas, the enhancement of existing parks and boulevards, and the addition of larger parks and preserves in the surrounding metropolitan area.[52]

Simonds's views on "Golf Grounds" continue his egalitarian notions of land use, as he debates the ethics of taking public lands, particularly portions of parks or forest preserves, for hobbies such as golf which cater to the special interest of a smaller group of people. He defines golf as "something to make walking interesting," but also sees golf grounds as opportunities for creating broad landscape expanses. There are mutual benefits, too, he believed, when golf clubs purchase and develop courses adjacent to public lands, where paths or other mutually supportive uses can be encouraged. Simonds created landscape designs for several golf courses in the Chicago area, notably the Chicago Golf Club in Wheaton (1894), the Glen View Club in Glenview (1897), and the Indian Hills Club in Winnetka (1914).[53]

Continuing his survey of landscapes beyond residential sites, Simonds turns his attention in chapter 15 to "School Grounds," noting that although many schools also serve as community centers, their design has received little attention. He argues that it is important to provide beautiful surroundings for "schools that care for children during the impressionable age from five to fifteen," when they would develop an appreciation of nature that could be lifelong.[54] College campuses are an important component of the educational experience as well, a belief Simonds expressed in his recommendations to Michigan Agricultural College (now Michigan State University) in 1906: "I would regard all the ground included within the area marked by a dotted red line on the accompanying map, as a sacred space from which all buildings must forever excluded. This area contains beautifully rolling land with a pleasing arrangement of groups of trees, many of which have developed into fine specimens. This area is, I am sure, that feature of the College which is most pleasantly and affectionately remembered by the students after they leave their Alma Mater, and I doubt if any instruction given has a greater effect upon their lives."[55] Today, that heart of central campus is one of Michigan State University's most treasured features.

Although he had no use for the traditional botanic garden—nature at the "back end of a farm" was at least as interesting—Simonds did believe that arboretums were useful as places to study individual plants and community groupings as found in native habitats. In chapter 16, he suggests that the arboretum contain areas of native forest growth to contrast the collection and provide examples of effective plant groupings. In this way, nature, the best teacher, could "even in the museum-like arboretum . . . give points on arrangement." Simonds used this approach in at least three of the arboretums he designed—the Morton in Lisle, Illinois, the Nichols at the University of Michigan in Ann Arbor, and his own experimental arboretum at Pier Cove. In each example he mixed natural habitats (existing or re-created) and planted collections, carefully fitting the design to the local physiography. At the Nichols Arboretum, which includes dramatic glaciated topographic features, Simonds carefully preserved existing landforms and wooded ridges, creating open meadows and placing collections in the valleys, which had been kept open for farming at the time the land was donated. He also carefully sited roads and walkways to fit the topography and reveal vistas as one walked or drove through the landscape.

For someone so prominent in the world of cemetery design, it is surprising that Simonds devoted so little space to the topic in his book. The chapter was written almost as a set of instructions. In fact, the "rules" adopted by the Association of American Cemetery

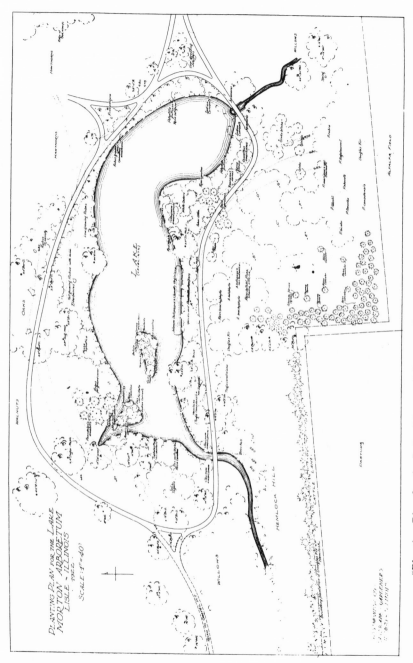

"Planting Plan for the Lake, Morton Arboretum." 1922. *Courtesy Morton Arboretum, Lisle, Ill.*

Lake Marmo under construction. Fall 1921. *Courtesy Morton Arboretum, Lisle, Ill.*

Early view of Nichols Arboretum. *Courtesy Nichols Arboretum, University of Michigan, Ann Arbor.*

Superintendents in 1890 are embedded in the text.[56] The creation of "places of rest and freedom from intrusion . . . the very best production of landscape art . . . may seem to exist more for the living than the dead, but," Simonds realistically noted, "the living are the ones that need them." It is interesting that both Simonds and his wife, Martha, chose to be cremated and have their ashes scattered under two beeches at their Pier Cove property rather than at one of the cemeteries he designed.[57] For them, perhaps a natural setting was more fitting as a final resting place than any cemetery—even of his own creation.

In the book's final chapter, "City and Regional Planning," Simonds extends his fundamental principle—looking to nature as our guide in designing our landscapes—to the broadest scale. He contrasts the then-current trend of the City Beautiful movement, which followed principles articulated by Daniel Burnham in his plan for Chicago emphasizing redesign of the civic center, with the English tradition of the garden city, which expressed a "mutual dependence" between city and country.[58] Simonds noted that many features of the new approach—such as diagonal streets—come at great expense. At the edge of cities, where new development was taking place, however, Simonds saw the "urgent" need for wise planning to "save a stream, a wooded hillside, an Indian mound, or other historic or natural feature."

Although the practical steps for achieving healthy city planning which Simonds lays out are grossly inadequate to the task, his ideas foreshadow the innovative practices widely accepted today in the increasing effort to solve the critical problem of "sprawl." Simonds argued for the absolute necessity of planning with reference to the natural features that make up a city's setting and region as well as with reference to its buildings, transportation systems, open spaces, and projected growth rates. As we enter the new century, designers are once again talking about the interrelationship of city and country from a combined ecological, functional, and aesthetic perspec-

Walkway, Graceland Cemetery. *Courtesy Landscape Architecture Concentration, School of Natural Resources and Environment, University of Michigan, Ann Arbor.*

tive, reminding us again, as Simonds did, that the "costs" associated with "intelligent study" are relatively small in comparison to the vast sums spent in wasteful construction and maintenance.

Throughout *Landscape-Gardening*, as in all of his writings, Simonds's fundamental theme is clear and simple: nature is the great teacher. He exhorts his readers to study the landscape intently, absorbing both obvious patterns and subtle beauty. In today's world, that charge is even more important than it was in Simonds's, as the remnants of unspoiled nature become ever rarer at the same time that our recognition of the need for biodiversity—nature in all its forms—becomes more acute.[59]

Simonds's philosophy echoes in one of the more vital movements within the field of landscape architecture today, which emphasizes the use of local habitats as models for a more sustainable approach to our design of the landscape. His knowledge came from a deep familiarity with these habitats, which he developed through the kind of direct study of nature he promotes in *Landscape-Gardening*. Our general understanding of plant ecology and ecosystems may be more advanced than Simonds's, but this specific, close experience of nature is as crucial as ever—albeit vastly more challenging to acquire.

With this republication of *Landscape-Gardening*, O. C. Simonds's ideas are given a new life and the potential to reach a new generation, one who faces the problem of the ever-increasing placelessness of the American landscape. Today, as never before, we are challenged not only to save and preserve what remains of native beauty but to restore landscapes that are badly degraded and maintain little relation to the natural heritage of their region.

One of Simonds's chief aims, as his obituary noted, "was to leave the world more beautiful than he found it and to teach people with whom he came in contact to be more appreciative of its beauty."[60] *Landscape-Gardening* shares the wisdom he gained over a lifetime of doing just that. This reprint carries his legacy into the new century.[61]

NOTES

I thank the following people for their help as I wrote this essay. Members of the Simonds family—especially Robert C. Simonds, Roberta L. Simonds, and Barbara Simonds Valentine—were particularly generous in providing materials and information. I was privileged also to be able to talk with the now late Marshall Simonds as well as other members of the Pier Cove community, who graciously shared their memories with me. Jean Whittemore Sharp shared materials and information about her father, Harlow Whittemore, and I received additional materials from Charles Cares, professor *emeritus,* University of Michigan. Scott Mehaffey and Michael Steiber at the Morton Arboretum assisted at critical moments. Previous research on Simonds by Barbara Geiger, Julia Sniderman Bachrach, and Jo Ann Nathan was an invaluable source. Robin Karson was immensely patient and understanding throughout. The editorial help that she and Carol Betsch provided has made this a richer, much more readable piece. Finally, my wife, Susan, was unflagging in her patience and support.

1. Barbara Geiger, "'Nature as the Great Teacher': The Life and Work of Landscape Designer O. C. Simonds," Master's thesis, University of Wisconsin, 1997, 131.

2. "Book Reviews," *Landscape Architecture* 11 (April 1921): 155–57.

3. The current movement for ecologically sound approaches to landscape design is perhaps an outgrowth of the late 1960s and early 1970s period, which saw the publication of Ian McHarg's *Design with Nature* (1969), Darrell Morrison's efforts to create native gardens in Madison, Wisc., the beginnings of the National Wildlife Federation's Backyard Wildlife Program (in 1972), and the founding of Wild Ones Natural Landscapers, Ltd. (in 1979). See McHarg, *Design with Nature* (Garden City, N.Y.: Doubleday, 1969); Bret Rappaport and Bevin Horn, "Weeding Out Bad Vegetation Control Ordinances," *Restoration and Management Notes* 16 (Summer 1998): 51–58; Kathleen Fisher, "Class Act: Landscape Architecture Professor Darrel Morrison," *American Gardener* 77 (January/February 1998): 22–27.

4. Mara Gelbloom, "Ossian Simonds: Prairie Spirit in Landscape Gardening," *Prairie School Review* 12, no. 2 (1975): 11–15. Gelbloom discusses the relationship of Simonds's ideas to those of Olmsted, H. W. S. Cleveland, Downing, Repton, and others.

5. Roy West, "Ossian Cole Simonds, November 11, 1955–November 20, 1931," *American Landscape Architect* 5 (December 1931): 17.

6. Herbert Simonds, *Reminiscences of Herbert R. Simonds* (self-published, 1968), 106. Apparently this story was frequently retold by Simonds. Another abbreviated version is in Ernest Stevens Leland and Donald W. Smith, "Ossian Cole Simonds: Master of Landscape Architecture," in *Pioneers of Cemetery Administration in America* (Association of American Cemetery Superintendents, 1941), copy in the Simonds Archives, Morton Arboretum, Lisle, Ill.

7. Theodore Turak, *William Le Baron Jenney: A Pioneer of Modern Architecture* (Ann Arbor: UMI Research Press, 1986).

8. Robert Bruegmann, *The Architects and the City: Holabird & Roche of Chicago, 1880-1918* (Chicago: University of Chicago Press, 1997), 10–15.

9. Ossian Cole Simonds, "Graceland at Chicago," *American Landscape Architect* 6 (January 1932): 12.

10. Bryan Lathrop, "A Plea for Landscape-Gardening" and "Parks and Landscape-Gardening."

11. Simonds, "Graceland at Chicago," 17.

12. Simonds discusses his use of the term in the first chapter, pages 17–19.

13. Simonds's efforts at Iowa State may have laid the groundwork for the landscape architecture program there; Michigan Agricultural College (now Michigan State) had a landscape horticulture program that pre-dated Simonds's efforts to establish a landscape design program there.

14. Simonds developed the lectures as a way of teaching college students to become intelligent and responsible citizens and designers who cared about their home places, cities, farms, and regions. There is still a critical need for this education.

15. The breadth that Simonds brought to his own efforts—formal training in architecture and engineering, lifelong study of plants and their habitats, personal interests in music and art, extensive reading in the literature, and wide travel both in North America and abroad—cast a model for landscape architectural education that has continued in programs today.

16. H. Simonds, *Reminiscences,* 19.

17. Ibid.,16

18. Thomas B. Curtis, interview by the author, May 1990; Jeanette Studley, interview by the author, May 1990; Geiger, "Nature as the Great Teacher," 52–54; Robert C. Simonds, letter to the author, May 16, 1999.

19. Jeannette Studley, interview by the author, July 1987.

20. "Illinois Out-Door Improvement Association," *Park and Cemetery* 19 (December 1909): 176–77.

21. O. C. Simonds, "The Aesthetic Value of Wooded Areas in Michigan," in *Michigan Forestry: Some Questions Answered Connected with a Vital Subject* (Lansing: Michigan Forestry Commission, 1907), 16–18.

22. Wilhelm Miller, *The Prairie Spirit in Landscape Gardening*, Circular no. 184 (Urbana: Agricultural Experiment Station, Department of Horticulture, University of Illinois, 1915), 2–4; Gelbloom, "Ossian Simonds," 5–7; Robert E. Grese, *Jens Jensen: Maker of Natural Parks and Gardens* (Baltimore: Johns Hopkins University Press, 1992), 44–51.

23. O. C. Simonds to Wilhelm Miller, July 20, 1915, University of Illinois Archives, Urbana; I thank Christopher Vernon for sharing this reference with me. Alfred Caldwell, interview by the author, December 17, 1989; Malcolm Collier, "Transcript of Interviews with Alfred Caldwell, January 1979," Jensen Archives, Morton Arboretum, Lisle, Ill., 8–22. Marshall Johnson, interview by Leonard Eaton, June 9, 1959, Jensen Archives, Morton Arboretum.

24. Robert Grese, "The Prairie Gardens of O. C. Simonds and Jens Jensen," in *Regional Garden Design in the United States*, ed. Therese O'Malley and Marc Treib (Washington, D.C.: Dumbarton Oaks, 1995), 104–5.

25. Karl B. Lohmann, *Twenty-seventh Annual Meeting, American Society of Landscape Architects* (Boston: American Society of Landscape Architects, 1926), 3–4. Jensen belonged to the ASLA for only a few years, quitting after the organization refused to reprimand the landscape architect who altered his design for Henry and Clara Ford's Fairlane estate; see Grese, *Jens Jensen*, 102.

26. Notes from the Prairie Club indicate that Gertrude Simonds helped to lead some of the club's walks, including one at Starved Rock State Park on May 26, 1911, which she co-led with Jensen. She also joined its board of directors in 1915. Prairie Club Archives, Chesterton Public Library, Chesterton, Ind.

27. Warren H. Manning, "The Citizen-Making Crafts of Illinois," unpublished paper, February 14, 1930, in Harvard Microfilms Collection, Loeb Library, Graduate School of Design, Harvard University.

28. Warren H. Manning, "A National Plan Study Brief," *Landscape Architecture* 13 (July 1923): 3–24. During the 1910s, Manning had published a small magazine called *Billerica*, which dealt with planning and design issues. For a time, he published an edition that focused on western Massachusetts as well as a "North Shore Illinois Edition," to which Simonds contributed an article titled "The Treatment of Roadsides along the North Shore" (4 [August 1915]: 7–8).

29. Friends of Our Native Landscape, *A Park and Forest Policy for Illinois* (Chicago: Friends of Our Native Landscape, 1926).

30. Liberty Hyde Bailey to Warren H. Manning, January 13, 1896, Liberty Hyde Bailey Papers, Department of Manuscripts and University Archives, Cornell University, Ithaca, N.Y.

31. Warren H. Manning, *A Handbook for Planning and Planting Small Home Grounds* (Menomonie, Wisc.: Stout Manual Training School, 1899); Warren H. Manning, "Landscape Gardening," in *Standard Cyclopedia of Horticulture*, ed. Liberty Hyde Bailey (New York: Macmillan, 1916), 1783–89.

32. *Standard Cyclopedia*, 1664–66. There are letters between Bailey or Miller and Simonds in the Bailey Papers at Cornell. Bailey apparently felt quite comfortable seeking advice from Simonds on various topics related to landscape gardening and asking him to write articles or send pictures of his work.

33. Carol Aronovici, "Liberty H. Bailey," *Survey* (March 1951): 126.

34. O. C. Simonds, "Landscape-Gardening," Lecture no. 1, February 15, 1909, Bentley Historical Library, University of Michigan, Ann Arbor.

35. "Mystery" as related to landscape preference has been researched intensively by environmental psychologists. Rachel Kaplan and Stephen Kaplan, for example, have developed a matrix to describe what they have observed to be key predictors of landscape preference. The two-by-two matrix includes legibility and coherence as factors of understanding, and mystery and complexity as factors of exploration. See their *Experience of Nature: A Psychological Perspective* (New York: Oxford University Press, 1989), 49–69.

3〉   ialons," *Country Life in America,* April
1914, 3

37. ı   ıde from the Landscape Architecture Progı

38. Georı   ıvid Lowenthal (Cambridge:
Harvard Univ

39. Gifford ı
Printing Office, ı
Page, 1910).

40. Charles Eliot,
People," *Garden and Fo*

41. Frank A. Waugh,
Extent and Character, with
to Methods of Development a
ment of Agriculture, Forest S
National Forests (Washington,
Service, 1918).

42. See, for example, Burton V. ь
Stephen H. Spurr, *Forest Ecology* (Nev
"The Level-of-Integration Concept and
larly, other modern scientists have pointeα   ɔnsideration of soil resources
as one of the key factors in plant failure, parι   ιy in urban landscapes. See Philip
J. Craul, *Urban Soil in Landscape Design* (New York: Wiley, 1992); James C. Patterson,
"Soil Compaction and Its Effects upon Urban Vegetation," in *Better Trees for Metropolitan Landscapes Symposium Proceedings,* General Technical Report NE-22 (Washington, D.C.: U.S. Department of Agriculture, Forest Service, 1976).

43. Olmsted, Olmsted & Eliot, *Flora of the Blue Hills, Middlesex Fells, Stony Brook*
and Beaver Brook Reservations of the Metropolitan Park Commission, Massachusetts
(Boston, 1896). In this report, Manning is noted as the principal assistant in the
Olmsted office who organized the survey work.

44. It is interesting that Simonds, even though his work was characterized as a
"prairie style," makes no mention here of the grasses or graminoid species so typical
of the prairie region. (In chapter 11, however, he does list prairie grasses in his suggestions for plantings along a "prairie road.")

45. Wilhelm Miller, *The Illinois Way of Beautifying the Farm,* Circular no. 170
(Urbana: Agricultural Experiment Station, Department of Horticulture, University
of Illinois, 1914); Miller, "The Prairie Spirit in Landscape Gardening," *American*
Magazine of Art 7 (September 1916), 448–50. See also the discussion of the "prairie
style" with relation to both Simonds and Jensen in Grese, *Jens Jensen,* 44–51.

46. Miller, *Prairie Spirit,* 33–34 ("The Illinois Citizen's Oath" and "The Prairie Spirit").

47. Simonds to Miller, July 20, 1915.

48. Although Simonds did not restrict himself to natives in his selection of plants,
he was certainly one of the earliest advocates of many common native plants regarded by horticulturists of his day (and ours as well) as little more than "outcast

weeds." See O. C. Simonds, "Landscape Design in Public Parks," *Park and Cemetery* 19 (June 1909): 50.

49. *Landscape-Gardening*, 190–91.

50. Simonds's thoughts here closely resemble Jensen's suggestions for the ideal section of the Lincoln Highway, which was intended as a "model" national highway. As a member of the committee that provided initial planning for the Lincoln Highway, Simonds clearly must have had input into the guidelines that were given to Jensen. See Grese, *Jens Jensen*, 106–7.

51. Geiger, "Nature as the Great Teacher," 85–88; Proceedings of the Ann Arbor Common Council, Park Board Minutes, 1905–1914, City of Ann Arbor, Parks and Recreation Division.

52. Dwight H. Perkins, *Report of the Special Park Commission to the City Council of Chicago on the Subject of a Metropolitan Park System* (Chicago: Special Park Commission, 1904), 80–105; Grese, *Jens Jensen*, 65–67.

53. See Geiger's extensive discussion of Simonds's involvement with the Chicago and Glen View clubs in "Nature as the Great Teacher," 63–67, 165.

54. This idea echoes his earlier plea to the Illinois Out-Door Improvement Association; see note 20 above.

55. Harold W. Lautner, *From an Oak Opening: A Record of the Development of the Campus Park of Michigan State University, 1855–1869*, vol. 1 (East Lansing: Michigan State University Press, 1978), 83–84.

56. *Landscape-Gardening*, 301–4.

57. Geiger, "Nature as the Great Teacher," 153–54.

58. Daniel H. Burnham and Edward H. Bennett, *Plan of Chicago*, ed. Charles H. Moore (1909; New York: Da Capo Press, 1970).

59. One of today's brighter conservation efforts is Chicago Wilderness, a broad-based coalition whose mission is to identify, restore, and preserve networks of endangered wild fragments throughout the urbanized region. See Jerry Sullivan, *Chicago Wilderness, An Atlas of Biodiversity* (Chicago: Chicago Region Biodiversity Council, 1997), and Debra Shore, "What Is Chicago Wilderness?" *Chicago Wilderness Magazine* 1 (Fall 1997): 3.

60. Erle O. Blair, "Ossian Cole Simonds," *Landscape Architecture* 22 (April 1932): 234–35.

61. Simonds's own legacy of design work across the country is just being rediscovered. At the time of his death, he was said to have practiced in every state of the union, but with only scant records available, we are unlikely to know the true extent of Simonds's career work. Barbara Geiger was able to document about seventy projects across the United States and Canada, including a few far flung in Maine, Nova Scotia, Maryland, Pennsylvania, New York, Kansas, and Florida; most were concentrated in the midwestern states of Illinois, Wisconsin, Michigan, Iowa, and Missouri. See Geiger, "Nature as the Great Teacher," 163–67.

The Rural Science Series

EDITED BY L. H. BAILEY

LANDSCAPE–GARDENING

The Rural Science Series

Edited by L. H. Bailey

The Work of Art. The landscape-gardener's canvas, the background for his work, is the sky. Against this he may see the earth itself. Against this canvas he plants trees and other objects to form a pleasing composition, and if he is wise he will leave a generous open space on his canvas for nature to fill in with clouds and sunshine. Mount Vernon; from an old print. Page 6.

LANDSCAPE-GARDENING

BY

O. C. SIMONDS

New York

THE MACMILLAN COMPANY

1920

CONTENTS

CHAPTER I

CHAPTER II

CHAPTER III

CHAPTER IV

CHAPTER V

CHAPTER VI

CONTENTS

CHAPTER XVII

CHAPTER XVIII

APPENDIX

LANDSCAPE–GARDENING

LANDSCAPE–GARDENING

CHAPTER I

THE AIMS OF LANDSCAPE-GARDENING

THE purpose of this book is to help make our country more beautiful. "Our country" refers especially to the United States, although in preparing the text the author has also had in mind all those parts of Canada in which climatic conditions, general appearance, and habits of thought are similar to our own, and he further acknowledges a sympathy with Thomas Paine's statement, "The world is my country." One's country includes all individual homes and the thoroughfares that make them accessible, all public grounds such as city squares, school and church yards, parks, cemeteries, railroad rights of way, golf courses, national monuments, parks and forests, all streams and lakes, all shores and all land upon which one may walk without feeling that he is trespassing. It includes the atmosphere, with its rain and sunshine, its fogs and clouds, its hail and snow, its storms and calms. It comprises night and day and all the seasons. It includes the rocks, and all material and living things within its boundaries.

Why seek to make the country beautiful? To many persons this question and its answer may seem unnecessary, the love of the beautiful is so nearly universal. To say that anything looks well usually secures its adoption or approval. Still, there are some persons who seem to be indifferent to appearances, and for them a few thoughts may be helpful.

Nature, from the greatest snow-covered mountains and broadest seas to the tiniest pollen-grain or smallest of spores, is beautiful and perfect. Happiness comes in largest measure to those who live in closest harmony with nature. It has been said that beauty pays, and this is undoubtedly true. A farm that looks well, other conditions being equal, will sell for more than one that appears bare and ugly or slovenly. A beautiful horse or cow, or an attractive dish or tool, will bring the highest price. But if one thinks of dollars and cents only, one does not get the full meaning of the word "pays." Beauty pays by giving pleasure to those who see it. One can help to make one's country more

beautiful by making its home grounds, its roadsides, its river banks, its parks, intrinsically better
in appearance and by opening the eyes of those
who fail to see such beauty as already exists.

The art that accomplishes this has usually been
called landscape-gardening, and is the youngest of
the arts. It was given a special impetus in the
latter part of the eighteenth and the first part
of the nineteenth centuries. To be sure, beautiful
gardens and landscapes have existed since the time
of the Garden of Eden, but the desire to create
beautiful scenery and to treat its creation in a professional way first appeared in Europe at a comparatively recent date. It was the result of the
effort to improve and organize the landscape. Repton, in the introduction to his "Sketches and Hints
on Landscape Gardening," published in 1795, said,
"I have adopted the term Landscape Gardening,
as most proper, because the art can only be advanced
and perfected by the united powers of the landscape painter and the practical gardener."

The powers of the practical gardener are such as
are common in all agricultural pursuits, and presup-
pose some knowledge of soils, fertilizers, tillage,
planting, spraying, and the care of plants in general.

The power of the landscape painter as applied to pictures formed by real objects, to the creation of landscapes, to the study, appreciation, and development of beautiful scenery is the distinguishing feature of the art now under consideration. What power has the landscape painter? He depicts scenery upon canvas. One looks at his productions and realizes the warmth of spring sunshine in a valley, the majesty of a mountain, the force of the ocean, the beauty of the pink glow of evening on the snow, the charm of woods, running streams, water margins, and open glades. One almost feels the wind, the warmth of a summer evening, the cool atmosphere of the morning, the dampness of a rainy day, or the cold but delightful beauty of winter. How does the painter get this power? He learns how to draw and how to use pencils, charcoal, crayons, water-colors, oils, and pigments in the schools, but his chief inspiration, the source of his real power, comes from the out-of-doors. He looks abroad over the land, his range of vision stretching away on nearly horizontal lines to distant points. His canvas rests upon the easel in a nearly vertical position so that he can glance easily from the object he is depicting to the representation of that object (Fig. 1).

FIG. 1. — THE PICTURE IN THE LANDSCAPE.   His canvas rests upon the easel in a nearly vertical position so that he can glance easily from the object he is depicting to the representation of that object.

The landscape-gardener works in the same way. He studies the out-of-doors. He looks at nature on lines usually varying but a few degrees from the horizontal. He notes the sky lines, the masses of foliage, the lights and shadows, the varying colors and shapes of leaves and flowers, the lay of the land, the reflections in water. He learns the things that make a view pleasing, and then when he grades lands, plants trees, shrubs, and flowers, introduces water, rocks, or other objects, he makes use of the pleasing effects he has learned to produce pleasing scenery appropriate to the situation and the locality. His canvas, the background for his work, is the sky. Against this he may see the earth itself, the ocean, mountains, hills, prairies, or forests. Against this canvas he plants trees and other objects to form a pleasing composition, a picture if you will, and if he is wise and has the opportunity he will leave a generous open space on his canvas for nature to fill in with clouds and sunshine, with stars and moonlight.

Nature indeed is a most helpful and willing partner in all the real work of a landscape-gardener, and also his best teacher. She teaches other artists as well, but for the one who tries to help her in beautifying the earth or in keeping it beautiful, she produces

an infinite variety of plant growth and plant-food;
she brings rain and warmth and sunshine; she
provides air to breathe and a stimulating companionship to encourage growth and beauty; and she
spreads a protecting blanket in winter.

The painter completes his painting in a few hours
or days. It may then remain for years just as left
by his finishing touches. The landscape-gardener,
on the other hand, must wait years for the picture
he conceives to develop fully. His conception of the
effect he wishes to produce may be the result of minutes or days of study. It is gained as quickly as
the painter's idea of his composition, and the time
required for recording his conception on paper is
comparatively brief. Sometimes the scheme he has
in mind will be worked out directly on the ground
without the use of drawings. The result he is
after is out-doors, and as it is usually produced by
living things — trees, shrubs, flowers, grass, and
various ground-covering plants — which necessarily
change, it becomes a moving picture. In other
words, his efforts result in a series of pictures or
effects resembling each other but gradually approaching his ideal. His skill will depend first on
this ideal, on his ability to form a satisfactory

composition, to imagine a view with lights and shades in proper relations to each other, with harmonious outlines and colors — in short, on his appreciation of beauty ; and next on his success in grading, selecting materials, planting, outlining open areas, lakes, woods, groups of trees and shrubs, the selection and placing of herbaceous plants, and in his treatment of water, rocks, buildings, and other objects that may appear against his canvas.

Certain rules should govern his work. There should be unity. This means that from a given point looking in one direction there should be one picture and in this picture some special feature should predominate. The rule of unity is violated when, in looking out of a window, one sees two vistas, two or more dominating trees, two lakes, two valleys, two hills or two mountains of equal importance. It is violated when a garden with bright colored flowers, pergolas and seats is made to compete with a view of the ocean. There may indeed be flowers in the ocean view, but they should be incidental, like clover blossoms in a meadow, the blossoms of apple trees, lilacs or locusts. Green foliage, rocks and trees may enhance the ocean view, helping to frame it or at least not competing with

what should be the main feature of the picture.
What is true of an ocean view would be true of a
mountain view (Fig. 2) or of a picture in which a
valley or lake, a lawn, a house, the prairie, a distant
city, or a church spire formed the dominating feature

FIG. 2. — SUFFICIENT UNTO ITSELF. It would be unwise to have an artificial
flower-garden or any other artificial feature compete with a view like
this.

(Fig. 3). There may be several pictures seen from
one point, if they are in different directions, but
they should usually be separated from each other by
some object such as a tree, a bit of woods, or a mass
of shrubs.

In landscape work the fact that the point of view

can easily be changed must be constantly borne in
mind. It may be a window, a veranda, a seat under
a tree or in a boat, any point along a walk or drive,

FIG. 3. — THE POINT OF INTEREST. What is true of an ocean view
in regard to unity would be true of a picture in which . . . a
church spire formed the dominating feature.

or any position one may be in while strolling about
the grounds. The landscape-gardener, therefore,
designs a great number of landscapes in one piece of

work, in all of which the rule of unity as well as the other rules to be mentioned will have a guiding influence. These rules also govern in pictures that are painted, in music, architecture, sculpture, and

Fig. 4. — A Lake Scene in Scotland. The island and the mountain are too nearly equal in value. If the island were shown much smaller in relation to the mountain the composition would be better.

literature. There should be balance (Fig. 5), but this does not mean that one side of a view should be just like the other. A tree may be balanced by a shrub, a rock by a building, a mass of flowers by a single blossom. A judicious arrangement of light

Fig. 5. — A Rocky Precipice Balanced by a Tree. A landscape-gardener is indeed fortunate if he can appropriate a scene like this.

and shade is desirable. In a well-designed landscape there should be harmony of shapes, sizes and
colors. A plant with foliage like the yucca would
not be pleasing next to a maiden-hair fern. The
leaves of pieplant do not harmonize with those of
the rose. Magenta flowers do not go well with
scarlet. A certain amount of contrast and variety
give life to a landscape but if used to excess they
may deprive it of repose. Repetition in landscapes
as in painting tends to make a scene restful.

Thus all the rules of composition that are applicable to paintings apply also to landscapes designed or appropriated by landscape-gardeners.
A painter sometimes speaks of the "heaven-born
ratio of three to two," meaning that the focal point,
the point to which the eye continually reverts,
should be three units from one side and two from
the other side of the canvas, and the same ratio
from the top and bottom, instead of being in the
center. The same ratio serves well in designing an actual landscape, since a tree or other subject placed directly in the center usually looks badly
(Fig. 6). The interest in any view is increased by
an arrangement which piques one's curiosity. In
illustration of this, think of woods into which one

gets glimpses leading to unknown depths, bays of
lakes disappearing behind islands or promontories,

Fig. 6. — A Glimpse Through the Woods. Compare
this with any picture in which a tree occupies the
center.

lawns partly hidden by projecting groups of shrubs.
These give possible opportunities for making dis-

coveries, and such opportunities compete with variety in giving spice to life. The shape of a tree, the graceful or strong arrangement of its branches, the outlines and texture of its leaves, the color and forms of flowers, the curves of the earth's surface, the reflections in water — are all objects of interest and beauty, but beyond all these in making a view interesting are the elements of curiosity and mystery.

While landscape-gardening is more nearly allied to painting than to any other fine art, in some ways it more nearly resembles architecture. These are the utilities. Architecture is concerned with many matters not particularly connected with beauty. These are for the comfort, safety and use of those occupying buildings. In like manner, landscape-gardening is concerned with walks, drives, gardens, fences, location of buildings, and other features having to do with the comfort, convenience, and use of mankind. There is a similarity also in the professional methods of landscape-gardeners and architects.

The grading of surfaces, which is an important part of the landscape-gardener's work, is not unlike the work of sculptors, while the planting ma-

terial he uses makes an appeal to the senses of smell,
taste, and feeling not made by the other fine arts.
In illustration of this appeal, think of the smell of
the rose, the woods, the meadows, the sweetbriers,
the hundreds of flowers of the old-fashioned garden, the taste of fruits, sassafras and all the products of vegetation, the feel of a mullein leaf, the
bark of trees, the velvety lawn, the polished surfaces of cherries, the breeze from the sea, the water
in the swimming pool, the snow and ice of winter.

Landscape-gardening, more than any other art,
makes use of the natural sciences. Geology, botany, and chemistry are of special importance, and
there is hardly any line of study that will not make
the landscape-gardener better equipped for the
work he has in hand and better able to meet and
discuss with his clients the many subjects that go
with the development of land. Even if one should
not intend to take up landscape work as a profession, there are few subjects the study of which
will do more for one's general culture. An appreciation of attractive scenery will add to the enjoyment of life, the pleasure of reading and to one's
interest in the history of the world. The Japanese
have professors of the arrangement of flowers and

this subject is taught in their colleges. The study of landscape, embracing, as it does, all that one sees out-of-doors, is one of the broadest of subjects. It is far more important as a fine art than painting, sculpture, architecture, flower arrangement and gardening, since it includes in a general way all of these, and its principles are those of all the other arts.

It follows, therefore, that the landscape-gardener works with his imagination. This is true in a greater or less degree of other men, but, for the landscape-gardener it is preëminently so. He must be a dreamer, a designer, an inventor, a creator, — a dreamer more than most designers because it may take years for his designs to develop. He not only dreams but he creates, working with land, plants, water, rocks, buildings, roads, and bridges. He puts two and two together, joining the work of the architect or engineer with that of nature. His aim is to produce beautiful outdoor scenery, the scenery that includes all one sees whenever he walks or rides through country or city. He is often called a "landscape architect," but architect implies building, working with lumber, bricks, stone, mortar, glass, metals, in short, ma-

c

terials that are for the most part rigid and fixed. The work of the landscape-gardener is largely with things that are alive, growing, changing. As Bryan Lathrop has said, "It is not the name so much as the idea behind it which is objectionable." To use the word "architect" tends to take away that freedom and gracefulness that should go with the development of beautiful landscapes. The term "landscape engineer," which has also been used, is even more objectionable than "landscape architect," since engineering is not a fine art, and, while the products of engineering may and ought to be beautiful, its aim is strength rather than beauty. "Landscape designer" is not so objectionable, since it indicates the character of the work undertaken by the man to whom it is applied.

A "landscape-gardener" is one who may be thought of as trying to produce a Garden of Eden, a garden which is purely imaginary but is thought of as the work of a Power greater than man and more beautiful than anything the present generation has seen. The aim of the landscape-gardener is high, and this term, while not free from objections, conveys the correct idea.

All of the various terms employed are objectionable because each contains two words. "Landscape" is common to all, and if but one word were to be used, "landscaper" would seem to be the most appropriate. It would be used just as is "painter." The "landscaper" would landscape a tract of land, a park or a home. His work would be "landscaping," and when finished, the tract of land on which he had worked would be "landscaped."

The term used in this volume is the one that has been generally adopted by those who have written on the subject of which it treats, among whom the name of A. J. Downing stands prominently, because the wide influence of his writings entitles him to the distinction of being considered the father of landscape-gardening in this country.

In the following pages the materials employed in this art and some of the general principles of the art will first be considered; and then the principles will be applied to the treatment of special cases.

THE ART EXPRESSION

The beginning of every fine art is hidden in obscurity. It has been gradually developed until it attained a great degree of perfection. It may be surmised that there was a time when men and women could not sing, and when there were no musical instruments. Probably the earliest representatives of the human race could utter pleasing sounds, but it must have taken a long time to develop tunes, to learn the harmony of music, and ages to perfect such instruments as the violin, the clarinet, the organ, and the piano. The devotion to music was such, however, that this fine art became part of the life of every civilized nation. Music is needed at most social gatherings and at nearly all religious exercises. It is necessary in war and in peace. It is capable of exciting emotions of patriotism, of joy, and of sadness. It forms not only a part of the life of a nation, but dominates, to some extent, the lives of many individuals and families.

The development of sculpture doubtless began in rude attempts, like those seen today among some savage tribes, and continued with the progress in civilization until it culminated in Greece more than two thousand years ago. While this fine art does not make so universal an appeal as does music, it nevertheless exerts a powerful influence.

The different styles of architecture have culminated at various periods, but each, during its development, has been understood and appreciated by all classes of persons and has really formed part of the life of the nation or nations where it came to its greatest perfection.

Poetry and the art of verbal expression kept pace with music, sculpture, and architecture, and at present no art exerts a greater influence. One can scarcely imagine a civilization without books. Literature, indeed, lies at the foundation of modern life.

Painting and the graphic arts reached the highest development they have attained somewhat later than the arts that have just been named. The development of the fine art of making pictures, in so far as they represent landscapes, is comparatively recent. Such pictures now form an important part of the paintings seen in art galleries, public buildings, and residences. They appear abundantly among the illustrations of books and periodicals.

Landscape-gardening is now in the process of development. One or two generations ago there were less than a half dozen firms following this pro-

fession in the United States. Even now, but a
small percentage of all the people know that there
is such a profession, and of those who have heard
of it only a few know what it really is. Before
it reaches its full development, it also must become
a part of the life of the people.

If, as stated above, this art of landscape-gardening is growing, what will be its final attainment?
What will it do for the people?

If properly guided in its growth, it will teach them
to see the beauty of nature, the beauty of this world,
of which many are now as ignorant as the ten-year-
old boy was of the beauty of sunsets before his
attention was called to them.

It will bring about a different spirit with regard
to beauty wherever seen. There are many who
regard anything which is beyond or outside of
what is generally called "practical" as something
foolish, wasteful, and effeminate, not realizing
that it is the beautiful which makes life worth
living.

It will open the eyes of farmers and their families
to the beauty that is always around them in the
sky and in their fields, and, if they possess them, in
their wood-lots, their orchards, springs, streams,

and hedgerows, and in the birds that delight in bushes and trees. It will enable those who live in the country to get far greater pleasure from life than many do at present, and will stimulate them to beautify their homes and take pride in their surroundings, their work, and their free healthful lives. It will prevent a farmer from renting his field or his barn for a bill-board to advertise someone's pills. It will teach him that he may have, if he will, during each day of his life, that enjoyment in the beauty of the country to which business men of the city look forward as the crowning pleasure of their declining years, those years when rheumatism, deafness, and other infirmities frequently prevent one from receiving the full measure of happiness that nature should give.

It will teach the city dweller, who, to a certain extent, is fond of nature, that it is not the part of wisdom to create beautiful parks and build beautiful drives or parkways and then border them with bill-boards. It will teach him to respect the wooded bluffs and hillsides, the springs, streams, river banks and lake shores within the city boundaries, and preserve them with loving care. This appreciation and care will also extend to the suburbs and will bring about a friendly relation between the people of the city and those of the country.

The full development of that fine art, of which this book gives mere suggestions and glimpses, should result in preserving the country's natural beauty, and developing real outdoor pictures everywhere until the United States becomes the most beautiful country in the world — more beautiful than any now imagined, and fully worthy of the affection and pride of all its people.

What of the landscape-gardener? What should he have in the way of equipment, aims, and compensation?

As to equipment, "all is grist that comes to his mill"; but he should have above all a love and appreciation of natural beauty. It is of advantage to him if he has been born in the country, or at least has lived a portion of his life in intimate relation with woods, streams, and open fields. The history of the world, as revealed in astronomy, geology, physiography, botany, zoölogy, chemistry, and the development of nations, is of value to him. The skill of the artist in various forms of expression is also of value — expression in words, in drawings, and in actual construction.

His aims should include helping his fellow men and women to live happier, richer, fuller lives; helping his country, his city, his neighborhood, his own home to grow more beautiful; helping everywhere in that material, artistic and ideal development that comes from doing things in a rational, thoughtful, common-sense way.

His compensation in a material way should correspond with that received by men in other professions; but in the satisfaction that comes from seeing and producing beauty, from breathing fresh air, getting outdoor exercise and all the delights that go with the country and the great outdoors and in the pleasure and satisfaction of doing helpful constructive work, no profession can vie with that of this new art.

CHAPTER II

The Saving of Natural Features and Resources

THERE has been a tendency in the United States, and perhaps in most countries, to use up or destroy many things that would have been of value to future generations. We have needlessly wasted, destroyed and burned up large portions of the forests that would have been of priceless value even to the present generation. We have needlessly worn out and destroyed much of the natural richness of soil and have allowed large quantities of it to be washed away. We have destroyed most of the fur-bearing animals and the game that was once so abundant. We have destroyed the fish in rivers and lakes. All of these facts are quite generally recognized and regretted, but we have not yet reformed. The destruction of forests goes on, and scarcely any provision is made for the future supply of lumber. The same is true regarding many other natural products. Even coal and oil are not conserved as they should be.

One feature of this country, however, which is being destroyed and which is seldom mentioned, is its beauty. This loss is intimately connected with the other losses named. A needless destruction of a forest often leaves a barren waste. Compare the primeval forest with the "pine barrens" that have taken its place. Compare a newly discovered creek or river with banks well covered by native growth with the same river a generation later when its banks are denuded of growth and the river as if angry spends its energy in gouging out the land on either side. Compare the shores of a lake as first seen by white people with the same shores after the trees have been cut away and their places taken by ice-houses and other protruding or obtrusive buildings. Compare the tree-covered hills of some of the southern states with neighboring hills that have been denuded of forest and have been eroded by storms until the virgin soil has disappeared and the ground is worthless.

The history of what is taking place in this country is but a repetition of that in other lands. In

France, for example, it has been necessary to spend millions to reforest mountains and foothills that had become worthless through erosion and to prevent the destruction of land below. Such destruction would result from its becoming covered with the material washed from above. The reforesting would bring back not only beauty but safety. Many countries once prosperous have become, through the destruction of their forests, like deserts and almost uninhabitable. The United States should avoid a catastrophe of this kind. The loss of beauty always accompanies the destruction of a forest. This is one of the many cases where beauty and utility are closely connected. The forest is valuable for the wood and timber it produces and for the protection it gives, but it is also valuable for its beauty; and this chapter would call especial attention to this attribute which it possesses, and base on it a plea for the preservation of woods. This plea would be for the protection of the undergrowth as well as of the larger trees.

In subsequent chapters attention will be called to the various elements of natural beauty. In this chapter a general discussion of the subject of landscape-gardening in its relation to the entire country will be attempted.

EACH FOR ALL

A man with intelligence, good health, energy, and an appreciation of nature can build an attractive home with pleasing surroundings, but unless his neighbors are of like mind with himself, he will not get the enjoyment out of life that he should. We are dependent on each other. Each should do something for his neighbors, which means that each should do something for his country as a whole. He should constantly have that habit of thought that favors economy, thrift, neatness, prevention of waste and a creation of beauty, for all of these go together.

We, the people who came from Europe, found this country with a beautiful forest sheltering wild life and protecting clear, clean streams and lakes. It was at first necessary to destroy parts of the forest to provide lumber, fuel, and land for cultivation. The destruction was carried far beyond the needs, but some areas of original forest still remain even in the older states. These areas should be guarded and preserved zealously. Their utility has been discussed adequately by professors and others interested in forestry, but more thought and attention should be given to the part these areas of woodland play in making the country attractive and in providing healthful recreation. When this is fully understood and appreciated, nothing will seem more natural than to add to woods by planting trees and shrubs along the margins of existing growth, by preserving the young trees that start in the interior of the forest and thus insure its perpetuation, and by planting entirely new forests in those regions not adapted to cultivation and the ordinary forms of agriculture.

The streams, once so clear and pure, have been polluted until they are often to be avoided. They have become muddy and loaded with sewage. Formerly, their banks were sought as places of residence, where now, in some cases, these banks would be the last places selected for homes.

To make the streams available as attractive landscape features, — to say nothing of their effect on health, — sewage and other impurities should be kept out of them. Here the work of the physician, sanitary engineer, forester and landscape-gardener are closely related.

The margins of lakes, once so beautifully wooded, in many cases have become bare and disfigured with huge ice-houses and other buildings. This is even true of the banks of many of our larger rivers like those of the historic Hudson.

In the development of water power, large areas of forest have sometimes been flooded and the trees left standing to disfigure the landscape for years to come with their skeleton-like trunks and limbs.

We have gone from bad to worse in the matter of bill-boards, frequently bordering with them the main lines of travel.

We have disfigured the banks of small streams and rivers and charming ravines with rubbish of all kinds. We have gone along the country roads, especially near cities and villages, and when we have found the most charming spot, perhaps a leafy slope leading down to a pleasant valley, we have said "Aha! here is a good place to dump our loads," and have proceeded at once to smother every vestige of vegetation with ashes and tin cans; then fearing criticism, we have stuck up a sign "Dump no rubbish here" and have left the ashes and the sign in full view for years and years, until perhaps Nature through her kindness has covered them with grape or bittersweet vines. We have done innumerable things to give the country an ugly appearance and mar its beauty, blind alike to both, and then have gone complacently on declaring that we are the salt of the earth and pitying the people who live in other countries.

If a landscape-gardener were called on to prescribe for the country as a whole, just as he is sometimes called on to prescribe for the premises of individuals, he would probably give his first attention to the farms, because they form a larger part of the face of the land. They are not only the foundation of wealth, furnishing food and clothing, but they also lie at the foundation of our national character, because many farmers' boys and girls graduate to the cities, and the farmers constitute a large percentage of our population. The farms covering such a large proportion of the area of the United States form the greatest factor in the beauty of the country as a whole. In treating the farms, the group of farm buildings would first be embellished with trees, shrubs, and flowers, and then attention would be given to the wood-lots, springs, streams, and other features of beauty. Incidentally, all farm tools that have been left rusting scattered about the fields would be brought to a place of shelter. The farmer and the members of his family would be taught to see the beauty of trees and other vegetation, the beauty of rolling fields, sky-lines, clouds and sunshine, for, strangely enough, it is the farmers who live closest to nature who stand in greatest need of an awakening. Then, with one fell swoop, away would go all the bill-boards that disfigure so many of the landscapes and call loudly and impudently to each passer-by and then stare him out of countenance.

Having landscaped the farms and destroyed the bill-boards, the next task would be to improve the appearance of the highways. The engineers would make the roadways, but the landscape-gardener would plant the margins, giving these margins as much thoughtful study as a good painter would bestow on his canvas.

The school-yards would also receive attention, and when the rural districts as a whole were made beautiful, cities and villages would next require treatment. Each combination of city school and neighborhood center would be given ample space for buildings and grounds. The borders of the

D

city streets would be planted attractively, and ample spaces in the most suitable situations would be devoted to parks. The beauties of nature — the streams, hillsides, lakes, and rivers — when they exist within or near a city, would be preserved as indicated in subsequent chapters.

The individual homes of the cities and villages, whether large or small, would become fully as attractive as corresponding homes in other countries, where even the smallest yard is usually charming.

The home of a laborer or mechanic may indeed be as artistic as that of his employer. There is no reason why a laborer should not have a hobby and become an authority, at least in his neighborhood, on some special subject. It might be some plant or class of plants which he would raise and value in his back yard, some plants grown for flowers, or certain vegetables or small-fruits. A hobby of this kind, having to do with life out-of-doors and the good appearance of one's home, is connected with landscape-gardening, but for fear that some will say that a laborer has no time for hobbies, the reader is asked to read the statement of an actual example, although, in this case, the hobby had no very close relation to landscape-gardening.

Years ago a Mr. Currier, living in a city in Michigan, worked in a foundry for two dollars a day, a day's work at that time requiring ten hours. At night he would go home with his hands and face blackened from his toil. But notwithstanding his long day's work, he found time to go about the country just outside of his city and make collections of shells. He also found time to carry on a correspondence and exchange the shells for those collected by others in all parts of the world, so that in time his collection equaled that of any in the state with possibly one exception. If a man working for two dollars a day with long hours could accomplish so much, why could not the laborers of the present time with far greater pay and with short working days be able to make a special study of botany, geology, or any natural science, or a study of individual plants or classes of plants, or birds, and by so doing make life more interesting for himself and his family, for certainly if he had such a hobby his wife and children would be interested in it with him.

With the beauty of the country restored, and that of villages and cities properly developed, there should still remain a large area, varying probably from ten to thirty per cent of the whole, in forest and state, county, and township parks.

Although the forest has several times been mentioned in this chapter, it is a subject of so much importance that quotations will here be made from a little book entitled "The Forest Waters the Farm," published in 1886 by the Forest and Stream Publishing Company. This book should be read by everyone interested in the welfare of the country. It is a translation from the French, and the quotations are :

"One should cultivate his field according to its slope and its nature ; on high ground forest, here some grain, there turf-land for pasture, and above all, should never sow more surface than he can manure."

"The woods keep the water, the water makes the meadows, the flock the manure, and the manure the grain."

"A country without wood is a house without a roof. No peace there ! Sun, wind, rain, and cold keep everyone in a turmoil."

"The forest protects the sloping soil. Where the earth is in danger from the waters, plant a sapling."

"We should never sacrifice the woods to the sheep

unless we wish to be at our wits' end upon the plains."

Bernard Palissy said in 1563, "When I consider the value of the least clump of trees, or even of thorns, I much marvel at the great ignorance of men, who, as it seemeth, do nowadays study to break down, fell and waste the fair forests which their forefathers did guard so choicely. I would think no evil of them for cutting down the woods, did they but replant again some part of them, but they care naught for the time to come, neither reck they of the great damage they do to their children which shall come after them."

The above quotations emphasize the utility of the forest, but its utility is so intimately connected with its effect on the appearance of the country that both of its attributes should be considered together. It is impossible to give too great emphasis to the importance of either.

The landscape-gardener would not diminish the development of water power. He would instead encourage such development, because it would save coal and decrease the amount of smoke. He would, however, have some regard for the preservation of beauty in developing this power. When necessary to flood land, he would have all the trees and stumps removed before covering it with water, so as to replace the river with a clear, attractive lake without stumps or other objects that would be ugly, and dangerous to boating. He would either save suitable vegetation along the margin of the lake to be formed, or plant so as to give this lake the appearance of a natural body of water. He would, of course, oppose the destruction of waterfalls so unusual in their appearance as to have attained a world-wide reputation, but there is so much undeveloped water power that some of the scenic beauty of waterfalls can always be retained.

The artist would not reduce the supply of timber. On the contrary, he would increase areas of forests, protect new growth, and prevent destruction by fire. When trees are cut for timber, he would have all branches removed and either utilized or burned where they will not endanger the trees that are left. He would cut trees low to prevent the unsightliness of tall stumps. While the removal of branches and trimmings would help to preserve the good appearance of the forest, it would also be a precautionary measure of safety and would probably save timber worth many times the cost of its removal.

He would not prevent the cutting of ice, but he would build the ice-houses in a location and manner that would prevent their being obtrusive in the landscape. This could usually be done without additional cost.

He would not prevent advertising, but would recommend it in a less offensive manner.

In short, the landscape-gardener would always encourage production. He would encourage those things that make for comfort, and while doing so he would always give a thought for the beauty of the country and encourage others to do so also, hoping that by so doing the country as a whole, the farming regions, the cities, the villages, the parks, and the forests would continually grow in beauty, and life become more and more worth while. He would encourage a fuller, richer, more enjoyable and useful life for each individual, and nothing would contribute more toward this result than the existence of beauty fully appreciated.

CHAPTER III

LAND

LAND is the basis of all landscape endeavor. It supports vegetation and holds in its hollow places bodies of water of all shapes and sizes (Fig. 7). From its declivities issue springs and through its valleys flow great rivers.

Land consists of decomposed or disintegrated rock or decomposed organic matter, or both combined. Rocks may be decomposed in place and form soil on the surface, as in Kentucky and Tennessee, or they may be torn to pieces through the action of frost, ice, and water and moved long distances, often hundreds of miles, as in large portions of all the states north of the Ohio River. The rock that has been crushed and ground by force of glaciers may be separated by the action of water into gravel, clay, and sand and the finer particles of the latter may be blown into great hills by the wind. The forces of nature have by their action gouged out

Fig. 7. — The Beauty of the Land. Land supports vegetation and holds in its hollow places bodies of water of all shapes and sizes. Rock River, Illinois.

great ravines and valleys, produced hills and plains, left high mountain peaks, made dry land and marshes, filled up lakes with plant growth and formed the earth's surface as it is seen today.

No sculptor can rival nature in producing beautiful shapes, shapes that are marvelous in their graceful lines and surfaces, that show by their wrinkles the effect of struggle and resistance, that indicate the passing of long periods of time. Man in his efforts to grade land to fit the various needs can do no better than imitate nature. If he wishes to produce beautiful lawns, he may give the land the graceful contour of the prairies and place that portion of it which is richest in available plant-food near the surface where it will obtain moisture, air, and warmth and where it will be benefited by the action of frost.

Since land varies so greatly in its origin, it must vary also in its composition; but all land contains elements suited to some plants. Some lands are rich in lime, and on this account are unsuited to the growth of rhododendrons, mountain laurels, blueberries and all the beautiful plants belonging, like these, to the heath family. These lands are, however, well adapted to the growth of certain grasses and clovers, and to the raising of many trees and shrubs that are exceedingly valuable in landscape work. Some land, on the other hand, is very deficient in lime but rich in nitrogen and in elements that give acidity. Such land will produce the beautiful plants found in bogs. It is suited to some fruits, to many of the heaths and to many mosses and plants of the lower orders. Even the poorest land will grow plants that make a beautiful ground covering, and any situation may be made attractive by selecting the plants which fit it; but if one wishes a special kind of ground cover, like Kentucky bluegrass, one must see that the soil is adapted to the plant desired. Its adaptation will depend not alone on the elementary substances it contains, but these must exist in proper combinations, and the mechanical condition of the soil must be such that air and moisture will reach the roots. In illustration of the different needs of special plants, a case in point may be cited. In a certain nursery, the rows of trees ran east and west. At the east end the soil was low, black, and of a peaty nature, while at the west end it was higher and decidedly sandy. A row of elms grew with great rapidity and vigor at the east end, but made scarcely any growth at the west end.

Some Norway maples in a row next to these elms, on the other hand, were very thrifty in the sand, but stunted in the soil that would commonly be called rich.

Another important fact concerning land intended for certain plants is the existence of microscopic organisms, bacteria and protozoa, in the soil, which obtain nitrogen directly from the air and supply it to plants. It is not at all unlikely that these organisms may affect the growth of certain plants in other ways, and that there is still much to be learned about these minute organisms and their relation to the growth of trees, bushes, and other vegetation.

The effect of the mechanical condition of land is indicated by the rapidity in growth of trees and of other forms of vegetation in newly filled ground. Such ground may settle from ten to twenty per cent. This percentage in the newly filled ground must, therefore, be taken by air, and would indicate that an abundance of air in the soil is of great advantage to vegetation. The larger growth upon land that has been shaken by the explosion of dynamite corroborates this idea. When plants do not thrive, it is often assumed that the land in which they grow is too poor, and, therefore, rich black ground is added or plant-food may be applied in the shape of fertilizers. Usually this is helpful, but, sometimes, it is like giving additional food to a sick person when he has already eaten too much. Sugar maples, red oaks, cherry trees, beeches, pines, hemlocks, dogwoods, wild grapes, and many other plants grow luxuriously upon the sands of western and northern Michigan, even on land so poor that it is thought unfit for agriculture. This simply illustrates how all land is adapted to the uses of the landscape-gardener. He may improve it for certain purposes and make it better adapted for the growth of particular plants, but often his best course will be to select such plants as grow on land like that with which he has to deal.

Land to be useful must be stationary; that is, it must not be blown away by wind or washed away by running water. To prevent light sandy land from being blown away, it must be thickly planted, usually with perennials having a woody growth, although many herbaceous plants are also useful in holding sand. Much can also be accomplished by planting to prevent land from being washed away. The damage to lands by erosion will be discussed further under the heading of "streams."

CHAPTER IV

Planting Materials

THERE is a remarkable variety of planting material. Even to give a list of the various plants would take more room than this volume can spare. Such a list would include trees, shrubs, vines, herbaceous flowering plants, ferns, mosses, lichens, and fungi. With the gradual development of the art of landscape-gardening, the number of available plants has largely increased. This increase is due not alone to the discovery of species before unknown or to the development of new forms and colors through hybridization and other means, but to the fact that new beauty is discovered in well-known plants. Thus sumacs, elderberries, hazel bushes, goldenrods and asters, once considered so common as to command little more respect than weeds, are found to be really valuable in landscape-making. The introductions from little-explored countries, as from China, have also added to our stock of desirable plants.

TREES

Of all available planting material, none is more useful than trees. They have size, gracefulness, strength, dignity, age (Fig. 8). They carry the sky line to a great height. They provide shade. Their leaves are objects of perpetual interest from the variety they show in size, shape, margin, color and texture. Their spring coloring may be quite different from that of summer, and in autumn they may fairly riot in their wealth of reds, yellows, purples, and browns. When the leaves finally drop to the ground, their beauty is not all gone, for they still have pleasing shapes and colors and might well serve as motives in designing carpets and rugs. The leaves are useful as well as beautiful, for they breathe and prepare the sap of the trees for nourishment and then protect the roots, preserve moisture and finally furnish food. This is but one illustration of nature's combination of beauty with utility, a combination that will be found more and more prevalent with increased study and observation, and may even extend to the landscape-gardener's work of designing parks and home grounds.

Some trees are evergreen, holding their green

FIG. 8. — THE FRAMEWORK OF THE TREES. The branching of a hawthorn — an interesting example of strength and beauty.

leaves or needles throughout one or more years, but even in these the spring coloring of the new growth may make a delightful contrast with the growth of the preceding year. Such trees give warmth to the winter landscape. The deciduous trees, however, do not lose their charm with the falling of their leaves. Note the gracefulness of the branches of the elm, distinguishing this tree even at a great distance, the beautiful light bluish gray coloring of the bark of beeches and the great strength of their branches extending straight out from the trunk. Note also the rough bark of the bur oak extending even to the young branches, and the pleasing curved outline of the top of the tree, especially in the spring, this outline being due to the light gray color of last year's bark and later to the light yellow of the expanding buds. The mere mention of the names of trees — the sugar maples, lindens, cherries, sycamores, Kentucky coffee trees, pepperidges, sassafras, birches, hickories, walnuts, honey locusts, thorn and crab-apples — will bring to mind some pleasing peculiarity of branching, texture or color of bark, or even the old leaves hanging to the branches of certain trees, like the straw-colored leaves on young beeches and the reddish-brown leaves on some of the oaks.

E

No attempt will be made here to give a complete list of available trees or to describe them, as that work has been so well done in other books, but one likes to recall the names of some of them as he would the names and faces of friends. If a reader's favorite tree does not appear among those mentioned from time to time, it must not be construed as a reflection on his tree, as there undoubtedly is a place for every tree in some location, a place where it will serve better than any other. Such a place may even be found for a Lombardy poplar, a soft maple, or a box elder.

SHRUBS

Shrubs are like trees in many respects. They have similar leaves, blossoms, and fruits, and they are interesting from the color of their branches or their manner of growth, but they are comparatively small and usually have many stems instead of one. There are evergreen and deciduous shrubs, and they may be planted for their beauty alone or to serve as a hedge or screen. In landscape design, shrubs are useful in many ways. Often they are employed to grade down the higher outlines of trees to the surface of a lawn or other low area. They form an attractive border for lawns and lakes. They help to "tie" buildings to their sites and give an effect of age. They may be used to separate bays so that one part of a lawn or lake will be hidden from another. They may screen fences, laundry yards, or other objects that should be hidden, but primarily they are planted for their own beauty or perfume. This statement will be sufficiently illustrated by the mere mention of certain common well-known shrubs, such as lilacs, syringas, honeysuckles, and roses.

When shrubs are used to form a border, or when they stand out only as individuals, the lower limbs should be allowed to remain and spread out over or rest upon the adjacent ground. To trim off these branches and expose the upright stems greatly mars their beauty. It is not expected that grass will grow under well developed healthy shrubs. When shrubs or trees are first set out, the ground underneath should be cultivated or pulverized with a rake or hoe until August or September; but after one or two seasons of such care, when these plants become well established, no further attention should be needed, especially if the leaves which drop in the fall can be allowed to remain on the ground as a permanent mulch. The

FIG. 9. — THE NATURAL SKY-LINES. If one thinks of the edge of woods along an open field.

lower spreading branches of shrubs help to hold the mulch of leaves and make a graceful border for the lawn. Any one who appreciates the beauty of this border will not allow these lower branches to be cut, and he will consider the digging of a ditch about a group of shrubs an unpardonable sin.

The value of shrubs in a landscape will be appreciated if one thinks of the edge of woods (Fig. 9) along an open field where the trunks of the trees are for the most part hidden with a natural growth of viburnums, dogwoods, hazels and elderberries, with groups of wild roses tucked in here and there, or when one looks at two buildings (Figs. 10 and 11) rising from open areas, one perfectly bare and the other partially hidden with a growth of shrubs, vines and flowers.

VINES

Vines are climbing plants, some woody, some herbaceous. They climb by tendrils like the grape, by rootlets like the poison ivy, or by twining like the moonseed. The ends of rootlets are often spread out into sucker-like disks. Vines are beautiful in foliage, — note any well-known species; in flowers, as climbing roses, morning-glories and honeysuckles;

FIG. 10. — Naked and Defenseless. Compare with Fig. 11, showing a setting of shrubs.

FIG. 11. — Clothed and Protected. Partially hidden with a growth of shrubs, vines and flowers.

and in fruit, as note especially bittersweet. Some are very fragrant when in bloom, for example wild grape and Hall's honeysuckle. Many vines, like the wild grape, grow with great rapidity and often smother the host that gives them support. It is dangerous, therefore, to plant them about shrubs, and caution should be exercised when they are near trees, for a vigorous grapevine will soon reach the top of the tallest growth in a forest. For covering trellises, lattice-work and walls, however, vines are exceedingly useful, and they often form most attractive ground covers.

HERBACEOUS FLOWERING PLANTS

Many books have been written about flowers and flower-gardens, but no description can convey an adequate idea of the beauty and perfume of a peony, iris, or lily, to say nothing of the rose. To obtain a knowledge of flowers, one must see them at close hand and know them by smell as well as by sight. They belong in every near-by landscape, where they may enhance the general effect, and also in the garden for cut-flowers, and in special gardens for the display of one or more kinds of bloom. There are hardy flowers, from the snowdrops of March to the asters and gentians of October or November. There are flowers of all colors, and one can devote a lifetime to collecting flowers of one type, as the peonies or the hardy chrysanthemums, or to arranging a succession of harmonious combinations.

One can have wall-gardens, water-gardens, wild-gardens, bog-gardens, and gardens of a particular season or of specially selected colors. These are intensely interesting. One can imagine how much interest might be taken in a garden devoted to hyacinths, to the various kinds of narcissus, to orchids, to peonies, to lupines, to columbines, to irises, to gentians, or to dahlias. These, however, are special interests and can hardly be entered into in detail by one devoting his life to the general practice of landscape-gardening. To do so would be like an architect's decorating the rooms of his buildings and painting the pictures for the walls.

FERNS

Ferns can be selected for nearly all positions, dry, moist, sunny, or shady. They are beautiful and interesting plants and should find a place in nearly every scheme for the development of ground along

artistic lines. Fortunately, many species are perfectly hardy even in northern climates.

MOSSES AND LICHENS

Mosses and lichens, using these terms with their
popular significance, are humble specimens of the
vegetable kingdom not usually considered as material
for planting. Mosses have, however, been transplanted successfully to many gardens. They are
beautiful and serve a useful purpose as a carpet or
as a setting for small flowering plants. A professor
from a New England university said a moss garden
in Scotland was the most charming thing he saw
during his trip to Europe. Lichens may sometimes
be transplanted successfully with the bowlders on
which they grow. Since mosses and lichens are
sometimes the most attractive plants seen in woods,
it ought to be possible to utilize them to advantage
in parks and home grounds.

CHAPTER V

Arrangement of Planting

The arrangement of trees, shrubs, and flowers is often of more importance than the plant selected, since it may make little difference whether a linden, a maple, or a tulip tree is chosen to carry the sky-line to the desired height, while the sky-line itself may be of the greatest value. Sometimes a mass of shrubs is needed in a certain place, a mass which might be made satisfactorily of viburnums, dogwoods or hazels, or a combination of these and similar shrubs. The arrangement of plants will be discussed in some detail under the headings of home grounds, thoroughfares, parks, arboretums, cemeteries, and school grounds, but certain general rules or principles may advantageously be mentioned here.

Hills may be emphasized or accented by planting tall-growing trees at the top, medium-sized trees on the sides, and low ground-covering material at the bottom. This is so evident that it requires no discussion, but, like many other well-known rules, is often neglected, so that a ravine or valley becomes filled with trees which are nearly level on top and thus loses its value in a landscape.

In like manner, the broader-growing trees and shrubs should be planted at the projections forming the boundaries of bays of foliage, and relatively narrow specimens in the deeper portions so that the bays will not be filled up with years of growth and thus lose their significance.

Excepting in the limited narrow strips for planting along the sides of roads and walks, the borders of gardens, and other inclosures and orchards needing continued cultivation, trees and shrubs should not be planted in rows. This rule may call for some discussion. It will be acknowledged readily that woods have a great charm for nearly every one who has the privilege of visiting them. What gives this charm? The wonderful variety for one thing, but that is not all; the beauty of the individual leaves and flowers, but this does not fully account for it.

The great size of the trees, the manner of branching, the bark, and the varying distances that one can see into the depths of the woods contribute to their charm, and yet something more is needed in explanation. This is the fact that no three or more plants are in line. Each individual tree or shrub seems to have selected its neighbors. Two may apparently be talking together or enjoying each other's companionship in one place, three in another, and then there may be a whole town meeting of trees or bushes. Perhaps a thousand pawpaws may be gathered together in one locality, a group of elderberries in another, a grove of beeches in another, and chokecherries and sheep-berries in still another. One old patriarch of a tree appears to have gathered his children about him. This lack of regularity produces an air of freedom that is delightful. The truth of the above statement may be shown by an example.

Some Americans were approaching a forest on one of the great estates of England. They remarked with enthusiasm before reaching it, "That looks like real American woods." On passing through the outer fringe of foliage, however, and finding that the forest trees stood in rows like an apple orchard, they were disappointed. To be sure, the fact that forest trees, mostly beeches, had been planted and had grown to be three or four feet in diameter was very interesting, but the anticipated charm of the woods as such was gone. It is certainly legitimate for a landscape-gardener to attempt to produce this charm. He cannot succeed as well as nature, but he can sometimes come very near to doing so, and may really succeed in certain details. The artist's saying, "It is the perfection of art to conceal art," is applicable to landscape-gardening and is certainly true. When rows and circles are discovered, art is not concealed.

What has been said in regard to rows for trees and shrubs is equally applicable to herbaceous plants. One should study a hillside or a rocky ledge covered with columbines, a marsh dotted with lady-slippers, a sandy ridge covered with lupines and puccoons, the carpet of anemones under a thorn-apple; there are no rows in any of these examples, yet where is the artificial flower-bed that can compare with them in beauty of arrangement?

Although this rule not to plant in rows seems so simple, it is one of the most difficult to carry out. If told to the man setting out trees or other plants, nine times out of ten he will fail to observe it. He will try, but his trees will be in zigzags (Fig. 12). The lines are there just the same, only one line has been moved half a space forward. It seems absolutely impossible for some planters to escape straight lines. To test for rows, one should look at a plantation from every direction. Rows make a composition look stiff and artificial. They are

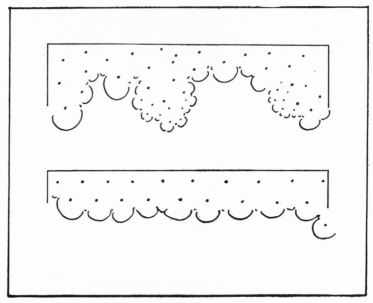

Fig. 12. — The Planting of Borders. Upper sketch shows irregular arrangement of trees and shrubs in border. Lower sketch explains an attempt at irregular planting which results in two rows. *Page 61.*

at times admirable, as in a body of soldiers, but they do not belong, or at least they should not take a dominant part, in the productions of those fine arts which have for their chief charm gracefulness and freedom. Arrangement does not depend

altogether on things that are planted.   Often it depends on things taken out.

"Plant thick and thin quick" is a good rule, since
it gives a good appearance from the beginning and
an opportunity for

preserving the
strongest individ-
ual plants.   The
thinning, however,
may not be con-
fined to things
that have been
set out.   Where
native woods exist,
the landscape-gar-
dener will surely
take advantage of
them in making

FIG. 13. — THE IRREGULARITY OF NATURE.
Usually dead trees should be removed, but
occasionally one is so picturesque that it
should be retained.   An old red cedar.

his plans, and he will do the same with any existing
trees or other growth standing in the open or extending along fences or old buildings (Fig. 13).

While nature is the best teacher and does some
things incomparably well, she does not always produce the most artistic effect, at least from man's
point of view.   She will close the edge of a wood so

tight with foliage that the eye cannot penetrate beyond the outer covering. She will soon grow a thicket that will hide the most magnificent view. She will grow a vine that will smother the most rare and valuable tree. In such cases, the judicious use of the ax will greatly help nature's own arrangement. Usually the poorer of two or more trees can be selected for cutting, but sometimes one's conscience will require the removal of a really fine tree. Usually a landscape-gardener is making pictures, not a collection of fine specimens, or a museum, but this will not preclude using the very best of trees when they are in the right places. Indeed a design may often be changed from that originally in mind to insure that an existing tree, bush, or group shall be in the proper place.

A view may be made to appear long by placing at its farther end plants having light-colored foliage, like that of the royal willow or the so-called Russian olive, and placing near at hand plants with darker leaves. This is only using the same device employed by painters, engravers, and by nature herself. Look at any photograph of scenery and note that the distant parts are indicated by lighter tones. This lighter tone of far-away objects is due largely to particles in the air. These particles reflect light, and the farther away an object is, the more particles intervene so that more light comes from the air and less from the given object. When air is very clear, as in certain mountainous regions, far-away things seem near at hand. On the other hand, fog makes objects look farther away. Fog often gives delightful effects by separating groups at various distances from the observer. It places light curtains behind near-by trees, thus bringing out their details of branch and leaf, and it hides the distance, producing a feeling of mystery like woods. This fact might be borne in mind in working out a plan; for the planting should be so designed as to be attractive in all kinds of weather. The arrangement of the planting and the selection of the material to be used should also be with reference to the seasons of the year and the hours of the day. The most telling effects may be desired in spring, summer, autumn, or even in winter.

Planting should be arranged with plenty of open space so that the plants may be seen and so they may be developed naturally and healthfully. The sky-line and the various outlines below it should be studied carefully and plants which harmonize

F

should be grouped near each other.   Usually a group should be made up of plants which come into leaf at the same time in the spring, as a shrub when growth starts late may look dead in comparison with early shrubs and one might feel tempted to cut it out.

One who aspires to arrange the planting for a tract of land wisely should study the plan carefully on the ground itself.   He may find certain unattractive objects to be planted out, like barns, ugly buildings, railway yards, and scars caused by cuts in hillsides or by white retaining walls.   On the other hand, he may observe that by cutting away some growth, a lovely valley may be opened to view, or a bit of the sea, a river, a distant village, or other objects of real interest will suddenly appear.   When this is the case, the owner of a small tract may really own all the land he can see in the sense that the pleasure of looking at it cannot be taken away from him.

To arrange plants properly one must know them, know how they look, how large they will grow, when they leaf out in the spring and drop their leaves in the fall, the colors they put on at various times, the date of blossoming and fruiting, and all the facts that have a bearing on their appearance.   He must know the soil each species likes to grow in and the slope most favorable to its growth. Arrangement is the very essence of landscape-gardening and may fill a lifetime with observation and study and also with pleasure.

CHAPTER VI

How to Plant

ONE may plant seeds, seedlings or cuttings, nursery stock of the usual sizes, or large trees with balls of earth about their roots weighing in some cases many tons. Doubtless the reader knows how to plant seeds : drop a seed, cover it with a little earth, sometimes very little, step on it and the planting is done. Few, however, would think of planting seeds to secure a grove of trees, not realizing how fast trees really grow; and yet there are oaks in the Arnold Arboretum at Boston so large that a man six feet tall can barely reach around the trunk of one of them at the height of his arms and these oaks were raised from acorns planted by Jackson Dawson within the memory of persons who are now of middle age. But to attempt to raise a forest, a grove, or even a group of trees near one's house from seeds would be a wasteful process from man's viewpoint (although not from that of squirrels, chipmunks, mice, and blue-jays that would eat the seeds) because of the uncertainty of the result.

Seedling trees are raised in a nursery where they can be protected and cultivated. It is often wise to plant these seedlings in permanent plantings, although it might be difficult to convince the man who wished to "see a tree during his lifetime" of the truth of this statement. A few facts in this connection may be of value. Small evergreens planted after a man was fifty years old have grown to be seventy feet high while he could still see them, that is during a period of about thirty years. Willows, cottonwoods, and soft maples have grown to three feet in diameter in periods ranging from thirty to forty years. Elms under favorable conditions will grow from one-half to three-fourths of an inch in diameter and several feet in height each year. Even oaks grow with considerable rapidity. Seedlings cost very little, often less than one cent apiece, and they will grow into trees worth dollars in a very few years.

Seedlings can be planted by sticking a spade into the ground to make an opening, placing the root in this opening, and then sticking the spade in the ground again and pressing the earth against the roots of the young plant. It may be well to carry the young seedlings with the roots immersed in a pail of water, and it is advantageous to have two persons work together in planting, one to use the spade and the other to carry the plants and place them in the earth. Sometimes it is best to cut the stems of the seedlings just above the second or third bud from the ground. The advisability of doing this, however, would depend on the kind of tree.

Young trees as well as old deserve admiration, and there is always pleasure in watching a grove develop.

PLANTING MEDIUM-SIZED TREES

Trees of nursery size, ranging from one-half inch to three or four inches in diameter, will of course usually be planted. Such trees can be dug with a good supply of roots and should grow, directly from the time they are planted, into sturdy specimens.

In planting a tree, a hole should be made somewhat wider than the spread of its roots and a little deeper than these roots extended below the surface of the ground in the nursery. Some of the soil will then be put back into the hole in a finely pulverized condition, and the roots placed upon this refilled earth at a height with regard to the ground's surface a little above that which it had before being moved. The roots will be spread out in a natural position and finely pulverized earth sprinkled in among them, the tree being given a gentle shaking as the earth is filled back, so that all the intervals between the roots will be well filled. When the filling is complete, the earth should be packed by treading around the newly planted tree. One reason for placing the tree a little above its nursery height is that the ground in its new position will settle, causing the tree also to settle, and when the tree is firmly established and the ground about it compacted by the settlement due to rains, frosts, and the passing of the seasons, it should stand in the position it would have occupied if grown from seed on the spot. No mistake is more frequently made than that of planting trees too deep. Sometimes trees that have died are found to be planted in a hole like a post with the crown of the roots a foot or more below the surface. Such trees are really smothered and have little chance for life.

Just before planting, the roots and branches of a deciduous tree should be trimmed; the roots being cut back to where they are fresh and full of life and the branches trimmed to reduce the number of buds in proportion to the loss suffered by the roots. Large branches ought not to be cut. Usually it is best to confine the trimming to a part of the last year's growth, so that the buds which start will be less than a year old. It is sometimes best to lean a tree slightly in the direction from which the prevailing winds come. The soil in which a tree is planted should be clean and the air which it contains should be sweet and pure. The earth should, of course, contain sufficient plant-food for the tree, but fresh manure, street sweepings, and decaying matter of any kind should be kept from contact with the roots. Leaky gas mains are fatal to any plant.

PLANTING LARGE TREES

Large trees should be planted only when there is some decided advantage in the immediate effect which they will produce. There are many places, however, where this advantage will exist. A new building may be given an appearance of dignity and age by the planting of a large tree, a tree one or two feet in diameter or sometimes even larger. The effect of a view in a park or a vista extending away from a house may justify the use of some large trees, which frame the picture that is to be developed. The planting of large trees or large bushes and vines is almost a business by itself. Various wagons have been devised for this work.

The important points to observe in large-tree planting are: First, to obtain the largest possible supply of roots.

Second, if the tree is trimmed at all only small branches should be cut, those not larger than the size of a pencil, usually a part only of the past year's growth. If larger branches are cut, they should be those in the interior of the tree which are unimportant and will not affect the general outline. When two branches cross or rub against each other, one of them should be removed. Any large branch which is removed should be cut close to the trunk or larger branch from which it springs.

Third, one should see that the tree is planted high, much higher with reference to the surface than it stood before being moved. This is important not only for its healthy growth but also for its appearance. If one looks at the trees which have grown naturally in woods or in open fields, it will be seen how the earth rises gently toward the trunk. This comes about with the enlargement of the roots, which raise the earth. A tree which meets the earth with spreading buttresses is far better in appearance than one which stands like a post. When the drainage is away from the trunk, the water from rains and snow settles in the ground where the fine roots are feeding and where the moisture will do the most good.

Fourth, to plant a tree is expensive. To prevent the waste of this expense, the tree must live and to insure its life it should receive care. The transplanting of a large tree is like a major operation at a hospital, where the patient must remain under observation and skillful treatment for some time after he is operated on. Necessarily, in transplanting big trees, large portions of the roots will be cut off, the fine feeding roots that are far from the trunks — the roots which absorb moisture and furnish the tree its life-giving sap. This supply of moisture of which the tree has been deprived must be replaced by artificial watering with a copious supply of water so that it will penetrate the ground to the lowest roots, not the watering which comes from a sprinkler, which only penetrates a fraction of an inch. To make sure that the water thus supplied reaches its proper destination, pockets or basins should be made in the surface of the ground above the roots to be fed. When a newly planted tree stands on level ground, such a basin will be circular in form, the deepest part of the basin being the circumference of a circle just over the outer ends of the roots, the ground about the tree forming a low, flat cone within this circle. When the tree stands on a hillside, the pockets must be so arranged as to retain some water for the roots on the upper side of the trunk.

Fifth, a large tree should be anchored against strong winds. Usually the ball of earth about the roots should be heavy enough to prevent the tree's overthrow, but as a precaution against unusual winds or tornadoes strong wires or cables should hold the tree in place by being attached to iron bolts or eyes screwed into the trunk high above the ground and anchored to heavy posts or other stable objects. Sometimes anchors like those employed by telegraph or telephone companies may be used. In this connection, planters should be cautioned against putting wires around the trunks of trees. Even when the bark is protected by strips of wood or rubber hose, damage is liable to result to the tree from an attempt to hold it in this manner (Fig. 14).

Sixth, when the newly planted tree is well established, the ridges that have formed the basins for irrigation should be removed and also the wires or cables that have been holding the tree in place.

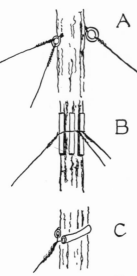

FIG. 14. — GUYING TREES. "A" shows best method. "B" and "C" are objectionable.

It is not necessary always to remove the bolts, as these will do no harm in the interior of the trunk. The growth of the tree will soon reach beyond the bolts. The surface of the ground about the tree where the ridges have been removed should be brought to a natural grade and then clothed with grass or other suitable ground-covering. The change to a natural surface may be made gradually so that the tree may by slow degrees become accustomed to its new conditions.

PLANTING BUSHES AND HERBACEOUS SUBJECTS

The remarks with regard to the moving of large trees are applicable also to the moving of large bushes and vines. The transplanting of all plants of woody growth should be during the dormant period, that is, when the leaves have fallen, in temperate climates usually from the beginning or middle of October until the following April or May. The expense of moving plants with frozen balls is, of course, much greater than when the ground is unfrozen, but occasionally this extra expense is justified.

Evergreens which grow in sand are more likely to succeed if transplanted with a frozen ball, but deciduous trees even of the largest size are successfully transplanted in fall or spring. The relative advantages of fall and spring planting vary in different localities. In some places, fall planting seems to succeed better than spring, even with such tender plants as Hall's honeysuckle; while in severe climates certain roses and other shrubs not altogether hardy should only be planted out in spring. Herbaceous plants should also be transplanted during their dormant period, but with them this period varies from June through July and August and around the year until March, April, or even May. The early spring flowers which utilize the sunshine of March, April and May before this sunshine is cut off by the leaves of trees and shrubs, often ripen by June or July and remain dormant until the following spring. These include blood-roots, trilliums, adder's-tongue and others which can be planted from July until the end of the season. Other plants which occupy open spaces and bloom later ripen and become dormant at various dates until the ground freezes.

CARE OF PLANT MATERIALS

Valuable directions for the preparation and treatment of the soil and the care which different plants require are usually given in nursery and seed catalogues, but some additional suggestions may be given here.

When one goes to unpastured woods or looks at the native growth along roadsides or old rail fences or stone walls, he sees plants that have no care and are generally healthy and vigorous. This condition should prevail and often does exist in tree and shrubbery borders. Groups of lilacs may easily be found which have received no attention for thirty or forty years, and they are vigorous and each year have good-sized leaves and an abundance of flowers (Fig. 15). This is true also of many honeysuckles, syringas, viburnums, and other shrubs, and is the ideal condition; but when trees and shrubs are first planted they need care until they become well established.

FIG. 15. — PLANTINGS THAT CARE FOR THEMSELVES. Groups of lilacs may easily be found which have received no attention for thirty or forty years, and are still vigorous and each year have good-sized leaves and an abundance of flowers. This is true of the lilacs shown in the above illustration.

The best care which can be given is to keep the soil well cultivated like that of a newly planted corn-field, or a well tilled orchard. With such care, young nursery stock will rarely require watering. If for any reason this cultivation cannot be given, a thorough mulching would come next in value. Cultivating and mulching are primarily for the purpose of keeping the soil beneath moist, and incidentally to kill the weeds which would rob the newly planted shrubs of food and water.

After trees and shrubs are well established, trimming is likely to disfigure them. The lower branches of shrubs are really the most important. They spread out over the ground, upon which they often rest. They help to hold the mulching of leaves which should cover the ground underneath them. To trim the outer branches, allowing only the central stems to remain, gives a shrub an unattractive appearance, making it look "stemmy." It is also bad for the health of the shrub, since it allows the wind to blow away the mulching and dry out the ground. Trees growing in the open seldom need any trimming to improve their outlines or appearance. Dead branches should be removed and trees should be trimmed for convenience. If they border a drive, the lower branches must not interfere with automobiles or other vehicles. If their branches spread over a walk, they should be out of the way of umbrellas, but a tree out upon a lawn, placed there primarily as a thing of beauty, should be allowed to grow in its own way, with its lower branches touching the ground if it is its nature to do so.

A very common mistake is to "top" a tree. To cut off all of the upper part of the tree not only disfigures it but often leads to its death. Thousands of maples, cottonwoods and other trees have been killed by this treatment because decay has set in where the trunks have been cut and gradually extended to the bottom of the tree. The trunk has thus been weakened, so that it has been easily broken and destroyed by storms.

Another exasperating treatment when it is necessary to remove trees is to girdle them and allow them to stand dead and naked for an indefinite period. Such trees excite pity for the tree and indignation for the girdler.

With thrifty plants and good preparation of the soil, the cultivation which has been recommended for new plantations will be unnecessary after one or two years. In orchards in which large fruit is

G

desired and in which a tree is forced to do its utmost, thorough cultivation may be required year after year, but with other trees and shrubs which are for orna-ment continual cultivation and spading of the ground defeats the object in planting them. Spading and forking up the ground breaks many of the roots, requires much labor, and the result is not beautiful. A mulching of leaves is not offensive even in winter when stems are bare, and the decay of this mulch will usually produce sufficient plant-food. Even when additional food is required, there are ways of administering it without disfiguring the surface of the land.

The roots of nearly all woody plants extend very deep, frequently to permanent moisture. When one looks at a hillside which is brown from dry wea-ther, the trees, bushes and vines are usually green and fresh looking. Occasionally, however, the trees even in a natural forest suffer from drought. When trees in home grounds, parks or other planted areas suffer from an unusual or protracted drought, water-ing may be necessary. In such cases, sprinkling will not answer the purpose. A thorough soaking of the ground down to the lowest roots is needed. After such a watering, a week or ten days should elapse before another is given. Large trees and bushes that are newly planted must have thorough watering if they are to flourish. Such watering, however, should not extend late in the season. Woody plants should not be made to grow in temperate climates after the first of September. The wood must be given a chance to ripen in order to go through the winter without harm. Peach orchards have sometimes been killed by cultivation which produced a late growth.

CHAPTER VII

WATER

THE land thus far considered in connection with planting and the development of landscape has been the ordinary well-drained land that is susceptible of cultivation. When there is an excess of water, various conditions may develop which will require special treatment.

MARSHES

When land is level or spongy, water may be retained, producing a swampy condition. Swamps are not unfrequently found at watersheds, so that water may flow from a swamp in two or more directions. Swamps in such locations are very useful in retaining water for supplying springs issuing from hillsides below and for keeping up a continuous flow in streams. Swamps are not only useful in this way, but they are often beautiful features in a landscape. They insure open space, across which one often sees a beautiful fringe of foliage. In the swamp itself many beautiful plants are likely to find a congenial home, among these being iris, cat-tails, many kinds of sedges, arrowleaf, cardinal flowers, marsh marigolds, pitcher-plants, sundews, swamp honeysuckle, ferns, astilbes, clethra, Joe-Pye weed and other eupatoriums, various grasses, and sometimes such showy plants as lady's-slippers and other orchids.

Marshes are often especially beautiful in autumn when their abundant vegetation and the leaves of surrounding trees and bushes are rich in color. There is hardly any better place than the edge of a marsh for the study of marginal planting. Here one sees interesting bays, delightful grading of ver-dure from the sedges to swamp roses, winterberries, poison sumacs, larches, red maples and giant oaks. A marsh is indeed often a second stage of a lake and sometimes conceals a lake underneath, when it is known as a quaking bog. To a landscape-gardener, the value of marshes, as of all other natural landscape features, lies in the hints and the suggestions they give for the treatment of similar situations.

If there is a piece of wet land on the area to be studied and planned, there are three obvious treatments to be considered. The wet land can be excavated, thus forming a lake, or it can be filled up, forming ordinary ground, or it can be retained as a marsh and developed by introducing the beautiful plants found growing in such situations. It would naturally be suitable for a bog-garden which can be made a beautiful part of a landscape.

SPRINGS

The waters from rains and melting snow which enter the ground at relatively high levels may descend until some impervious stratum is reached, and then flow out as springs where the impervious stratum meets a ravine, a valley, or the bank of a stream. Springs vary in size from a tiny trickling rill that will merely moisten the earth to a large river which issues from its source in such volume as to be navigable from its beginning; but whatever its size, a spring may be an interesting feature in a landscape. The smallest one may moisten the earth enough for marsh marigolds, forget-me-nots and iris, those somewhat larger may spread out into clear pools, reflecting jewel-weeds and gentians, or may tumble over bowlders and make cheerful sounds. A spring is an acquisition to be prized. Its treatment calls for some skill. It should either appear as nature's own production, as though man had done nothing to it, or, if some visible work of man's is necessary, this should seem to serve the spring and be subordinate to it. Springs that have sufficient fall and volume may be valuable as sources of water supply, either through gravity when at a sufficiently high elevation, or when lower by means of hydraulic rams or other pumping devices.

Some shade goes well with a spring, the two together producing a grateful effect of coolness on a hot summer day. Overhanging lindens, birches, hemlocks, alders, red maples and red-branched dogwoods seem appropriate for producing shade, but any tree or shrub leaning out from a bank immediately above a spring makes an effect which an artist would like to sketch. A spring may give individuality to a home, a park, a city square, a country road or a city street.

When the water supply is artificial and the water is forced from manifestly artificial forms, the spring becomes a fountain. Fountains of many different forms have been used from time immemorial and often make delightful features of buildings and terraces. The beauty of a spring, however, would seem to justify its introduction into scenery even when the water must be supplied by some prosaic pump. The pump, however, should be located in the city waterworks or some distant building or hidden underground, and the water come from an unseen source and be given the appearance of a natural flow.

STREAMS

The water from springs unites with surface water from rains and snow to form at first small streams, which in turn unite to form larger ones, and these again unite to form rivers. Small streams, known as rivulets, brooks, creeks, and runs, are very interesting features when they exist as nature made them. They are not only interesting in a landscape, but they frequently have waterfalls and rapids that make sounds pleasing to the ear. When first discovered, they are supplied with clear water as a rule and are bordered with vegetation which includes mosses, liverworts, many kinds of herbaceous plants, vines, and overhanging bushes. Sometimes they spread out to form placid pools, and again they are crowded in narrow gorges through which they rush with great energy. Such clear limpid streams usually are found in the country, seldom in a village or a city, but they might be kept clear, sparkling, and most attractive even in a thickly settled community.

Cities support large parks for the recreation and pleasure of their inhabitants. They have costly parkways or boulevards. Why should they not also have delightful walks? Walking is said to be the most healthful of exercises. It is certainly the least expensive, and the border of a small stream extending through a parkway would be a most interesting place for a walk. The bordering vegetation might be retained. The parkway might fit the topography, being narrow where the land on either side was useful for buildings or home grounds, and wider where the stream ran through a ravine or a valley unfitted without great expense for buildings or homes. In many cases, such a parkway might be accessible only by means of the path just proposed. In other cases, when width and direction warranted, a drive might be made in addition to the path. Speaking from a practical standpoint, a development of this kind might add many dollars to the value of real estate on either side, instead of depreciating these values by having the banks of the stream serve as a dumping place for ashes, tin cans and other refuse.

The writer can recall streams, usually known by

such names as "Cold Brook," and "Silver Creek," which once were as beautiful as nature could make. They were in the country near a growing city. Gradually the native growth along their borders was all destroyed. Then the areas of bordering land became pastures and the streams during high water began to wash away the land on either side, so that they grew more and more crooked and the bare earth exposed gave them an unsightly appearance. Then streets were developed near them, and their banks were further disfigured by the dumping of refuse of all kinds. This was often done clandestinely in spite of warning signs, the refuse including not only ashes and tin cans mentioned above, but old bed springs, broken dishes, furniture and dead animals. Finally the streams were replaced with large sewers and so the beauty of the original charming features of the native landscape was lost, save in memory, to the present generation, and lost completely to all future inhabitants.

Cities are willing to spend liberally, even medium-sized cities spending hundreds of thousands of dollars and larger cities not hesitating at millions, for the purpose of developing great parks. Such expendi-

tures are in accordance with good judgment and
wise foresight, but the retention of open running
streams with all the beauty originally found
along their margins would be just as wise. Walks
along the borders of such streams in going to
and from one's work would give a daily pleasure
(Fig. 16). Seats arranged within sound of a water-
fall or commanding a view along a stretch of
running water fringed with overhanging willows
would make ideal resting places. Occasionally
such streams are found within the boundaries of
great parks, and although these parks are developed
for the production and preservation of beautiful
scenery, they contain no features more attractive
than these lively brooks. Why not keep such features (active running streams) in intimate relation
with the homes of a great city? They require but
little land, scarcely more than the parkway along
the side of a broad street. If properly treated, the
care would be inexpensive and the appreciation thus
shown for nature would make a valuable reputation
for any community (Fig. 17).

What has been stated about small streams can
be said with even greater force of larger ones. They
may have been innocent, harmless and beautiful

Fig. 16. — The Water in the Landscape. One of the streams as beautiful as nature can make. Small streams when first discovered are supplied with clear water and bordered with vegetation.

when the country was new, but with its development, with the cutting away of woods and the denuding of their banks, they become destructive and dangerous. Often the bottom lands of medium-sized streams become waste land after the destruction of the forest.

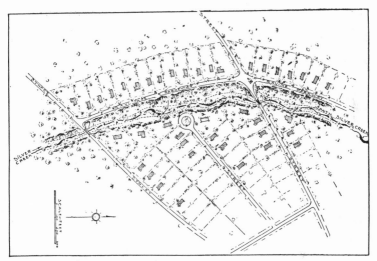

Fig. 17. — The Utilizing of a Stream. Sketch showing parkway in city following course of brook.

The freshets gouge out the banks and hillsides confining the stream, and distribute the material, sand, gravel, and clay, upon the flooded land, making it useless for agriculture. The swollen creeks and rivers tear out bridges, causing great loss and inconvenience. The bottom land is really rich in plant-food, and usually has abundant moisture. The valleys are warm in summer, so that trees grow to great size. If it was merely a question of dollars, a forest growth covering the bottom lands and steep hillsides along our smaller rivers would have paid well, since the value of the yearly growth would be more than an ordinary farm crop. But one should also consider the beauty which such a growth would insure.

As seen from a balloon or flying machine, the courses of streams would be shown by the irregular growth of forest. As observed from adjoining farms, there would be bays and promontories of foliage, giving pleasing lights and shadows. There would be a beautiful sky-line.

The bordering growth would show at the extreme height the tops of oaks, tulip trees, elms, maples, ash trees of various kinds, sycamores, beeches, lindens, which, in any of the middle states, might reach a height of over one hundred feet and have trunks with diameters ranging from three to five feet. The lower growth would include ironwoods, blue beeches, thorn-apples, crab-apples, red-buds, dogwoods, viburnums, hazel bushes, elderberries, roses, wild crabs, Virginia creepers, bittersweet, goldenrod, asters, and other plants, producing a growth so beautiful that it would be the envy of the designers and frequenters of public parks.

If forest belts of this kind, extending along all the streams, could be public property under the control of an able man, with the help of intelligent and enthusiastic assistants, it would be a great asset for

FIG. 18. — THE SAVING OF THE WATERWAY. Sketch showing bird's-eye view of wooded growth along borders of a stream.

a country (Fig. 18). The gain to adjoining farms would be greater than the loss. All neighborhoods would have comparatively near at hand beautiful park-like areas to visit for a holiday. There would be picnic places, swimming holes, canoe courses, fishing, and a chance to study wild growth. Such areas would be refuges for birds and wild flowers. They would furnish places for studying many things that would add interest to life. They would perpetuate for future generations the many natural charms which have delighted the boys and girls of the past generation, charms which are now lost in many places, but which might be restored with advantage.

The assistants who would have charge of definite stretches of the river forests just described would be equipped for their work by being especially trained as landscape-gardeners and foresters. The two professions can well be combined in one for work of this kind. An assistant with this training might have charge of a stretch of many miles of forest bordering our waterways. He would direct laborers who would grow to love their work. This work would consist in cutting certain trees and shrubs, the removal of which would improve the general effect or benefit the better trees and shrubs which remained. The material cut would in many cases produce firewood, which would have some value, and at times trees which had reached maturity would be cut for saw logs which would produce good lumber. The small branches and refuse could be burned on adjoining farms, where the ashes would make a good fertilizer. It is hardly to be expected that such forests would be self-supporting, but they would cost so little that the pleasure they would give would be obtained at a very low price. The forest growth would protect the river banks and hillsides and also the bridges and roads, probably saving each township far more than the cost of maintenance.

Larger rivers, where they pass through cities, should be bordered with streets. Their banks would then be controlled by the city authorities and might be placed under the supervision of park commissioners. The buildings fronting such streets would have the advantage of beautiful scenery. Many instances might be given of the added value to real estate commanding views of attractive landscapes. For office buildings, the better class of shops, and many public buildings, locations on these river streets might be decidedly advantageous. Strangers visiting cities, as well as the inhabitants, often seek the bridges to look up and down the river. The arrangement just described with well planted river banks furnishing a setting for good buildings would be a great improvement over what is frequently seen. Too often the banks are entirely denuded of vegetation and strewn with pieces of tin, broken crockery, ashes and cinders

H

and other refuse dumped from the rear end of stores, factories and other buildings which face away from the river (Figs. 19 and 20).

For certain kinds of business, it is true that some concentration of traffic is desirable; that streets

Fig. 19. — The Spoiling of the Rivers. Large rivers where they pass through cities should be bordered with streets. Their banks would then be controlled by the city authorities and might be placed under the supervision of park commissioners.

should not be too wide; that one-sided streets are objectionable and that city squares which make such streets really depreciate values. Nevertheless, there is a value in broad open spaces, a value not always appreciated. An occupant of an office takes delight in a view to the country, to the ocean or other large body of water, or to any clear extensive space.

It is one of the attributes of a river that it preserves an unobstructed stretch of opening. This space should count as one of the assets of a city. How

can it be made most effective? If a street extends
along each side of the river, all the persons using
these streets will have long views up and down its
course, views whose interest may be enhanced by
well-designed bridges or by beautiful buildings with
groups of trees, belts of shrubs, vines and herbaceous
plants so arranged as to frame in or make a setting

FIG. 20. — THE VIOLATION OF BEAUTY. A large river which passes through
the center of a flourishing city with a large population. The refuse-
covered bank is typical of many American cities.

for the objects and spaces one wishes to see. These
river streets might extend into the country as river
roads and have the advantage of attractive scenery,
easy grades and directness. Such locations are frequently selected by engineers for railroads, and they
would be equally advantageous for pleasure driving
and ordinary traffic (Fig. 21). Streets are like
rivers in preserving long stretches of open space.
When the street spaces are separated from the

Fig. 21. — Utilizing the River-Side. The bank of a river is as suitable for a road as for a railway.

river space, they add nothing to the effectiveness
of the latter. This is the case where buildings
intervene. On the other hand, where the street
spaces join that of the river, they add materially
to its value in the landscape.

The arrangement recommended need not interfere
with using the river as a source of power, since the
power can easily be carried on a wire to any suitable
place for a factory. The construction of dams,
while interfering with the effect of running water,
may sometimes substitute for this the reflections of
still water and a desirable place for boating. When
a dam is placed above a city and the water of the
river is carried in a canal to some lower point for the
development of power, the normal flow of water
through the river channel below the dam is, of course,
reduced. Some compensation for this loss of river
beauty due to lack of water might be obtained by
separating the river-bed into deeper channels and
islands, the latter to be planted with low-growing
willows or other forms of vegetation that would not
be injured by occasional freshets. The river-bed
would thus become a kind of water park on which
one would look from the bordering streets and from
the bridges. If a dam is placed below a city, the

river, where crossed by bridges and bordered by streets, becomes like a lake in having comparatively still water which will reflect the arches and the foliage flanking the abutments and covering the earth embankments or hanging over the walls that stretch from bridge to bridge.

In some ways, a dam below a city is preferable to one above. It saves the expense of a canal and the bridges that span it. It allows the bordering streets to lie close to the embankment where they will command the best views. It provides boating close at hand where employees and others could get delightful exercise even during the brief hour or so allowed for luncheon. It would also furnish a place for swimming. Since the level of the water would be reasonably stationary, the effect of the overhanging branches of groups of trees and the bordering foliage of shrubs and vines would be most satisfactory.

There are, to be sure, waterfalls, sometimes near cities, where scenic value far outweighs that of any power that may be developed. Such value should be preserved, a thing most difficult to accomplish, because scenic value does not put dollars into the pockets of those who most appreciate it.

The urgent plea which this book would make is

for the recognition and preservation of the beauty of all streams both large and small, in the country and in the cities as well. In cities, watercourses and their borders should become a part of the park systems, usually the most interesting and useful as well as the least expensive in maintenance. Such recognition of beauty and the preservation of river scenery would show that all men and women do not live for dollars, but that they love beauty, the most satisfactory and all-pervading attribute of this world.

The development of water power is to be commended. When a ton of coal is burned, there is one ton less in the world's reserve, but when the power of falling water is utilized, nothing is taken from the future because the supply of water is continually replenished. When coal is burned, the atmosphere is usually polluted with smoke and the beauty of the scenery injured or destroyed. The development of water power does not affect air, but it does often injure scenery by flooding and killing trees along the banks of the rivers that are utilized by the construction of dams. The engineer who is skillful in the construction of dams and the installation of turbines and generators is not always appreciative of the beauty of running water and tree-covered banks. His work should always be undertaken with the advice and assistance of an able landscape-designer. River scenery has real value and should not be destroyed without substituting in its place scenery of equal or greater value. Rivers are not only attractive features in a landscape but they serve for recreation in many ways. Their use as sources of power should not destroy their other possibilities. There are cases in which the recreational value is far greater than any utilitarian one, and the destruction of the former for the sake of the latter is a loss.

LAKES

Like rivers, lakes are naturally beautiful. Their shores are so shaped as to withstand the action of water and ice. The vegetation along their margins is generally pleasing when they are first discovered. The outlines given them by nature are nearly always satisfactory. The natural beauty of lakes, however, like that of rivers, is subject to dangers on account of the utilitarian possibilities of these bodies of still water. Perhaps the greatest injury to their general appearance is due to the construction of ice-houses. These are often unnecessarily obtrusive. If they were placed some distance back from the water and subordinated in the landscape by planting willows or other suitable trees on each side, they would not be so objectionable.

The next feature most destructive of lake scenery is the construction of boat-houses extending out into the water; and hardly less injurious to the appearance of water margins are the concrete and masonry walls which give a light-colored scar to the otherwise peaceful and quiet margins. The summer cottages also frequently destroy the attraction which has drawn their owners to lake borders. The most obvious remedy for the unsightliness caused by the structures mentioned is to place such as are necessary back from the shore. A boat-house set back in a bank or inlet need not be ugly. An ice-house is difficult to manage in a landscape on account of its large size, but much can be done to mitigate its usual ugliness by selecting a proper location and subordinating it by planting near it trees that attain great breadth and height. The walls along the shore are usually unnecessary and should be omitted. A summer cottage can be so placed that with proper staining or painting and suitable planting, it will be quite

unobtrusive and still allow its occupants to enjoy
the most delightful views over the water. When
walls along the shore are really necessary, they
often can be constructed with bowlders placed ir-
regularly upon a slanting surface. When the action of the waves is so strong as to make the use
of cement necessary, this material can frequently
be employed so it will not be seen by placing upon
it bowlders and gravel and planting shrubs or vines
just above it.

The study of natural lakes will help in the construction of artificial lakes and ponds. Natural
lakes have been formed by glaciers which gouge
out basins and then recede and leave glacial lakes,
or by rivers which change their course and leave
bodies of water in their former channels, or by the
obstruction of streams, or by any hollow land surface which catches and holds water. The natural
water supply may be springs, streams, or merely
rain and melting snow. The features to be studied
are the general outlines, the shores and the border
growth. A lake becomes interesting when one portion is hidden from another. The object which
separates the two portions may be a hill, a rise of
ground, or a growth of trees and bushes. The

effect desired may sometimes be obtained even when the water's edge is nearly straight by variation in a marginal growth. A tree or a group of trees may send branches out over the water to a distance of twenty to thirty feet, and next to such a group the ground may be covered merely with small bushes and vines. Thus the bank of a lake which fills an abandoned river-bed and is somewhat canal-like in outline, may become by suitable planting extremely interesting.

Natural lakes have usually been in existence a long time. Their shores have, therefore, become fixed and the slopes of these shores indicate the shape best adapted to resisting wave action. Rocky banks show the best form for an artificial barrier of this kind. The distribution of bowlders along natural shores should be studied to learn how to make the best use of such material in artificial lakes.

A border growth of trees and bushes often occurs where banks are steep, showing how to protect hillsides or abrupt banks from being washed away or undermined by water. Cat-tails, pickerel-weed, sedges and other growth along water margins indicate the conditions favorable to such growth. One goes to natural lakes to study the treatment of such water, just as one would consult a man of long experience in any given line for information gained by such experience.

Artificial lakes. — In the development of home grounds, parks and other open spaces, it may be taken for granted that still bodies of water will be introduced when conditions are favorable. The mirror-like surfaces of lakes and ponds give new beauty to their surroundings (Fig. 22). They show the light of the sun and moon and on still nights even that of the stars. They reflect the hills and clouds, the overhanging trees and vine-covered banks. They beautify the landscape and may serve as places for swimming, fishing, boating, and skating.

When are conditions favorable? The first requisite is a supply of water, and the second a suitable location. The water may come from springs, streams, or wells. In the latter case, objection may be made to the cost of pumping, but when there is an abundant supply of ground water, the amount spent in securing it to supply a lake will usually give more pleasure than that expended in any other way. Spring water is most satisfactory since it costs nothing and is free from sediment. The

FIG. 22. — THE LAKE IN THE LANDSCAPE. An artificial lake showing reflections of foliage and clouds.

water from streams may bring large quantities of sediment, especially during storms and thawing weather, and so gradually fill up a lake and cause a muddy appearance. Several remedies for this difficulty may be suggested. A border of perennial vegetation along the route of any stream before it reaches a proposed lake may keep its water clear. (See page 88.) The water of a stream may be diverted during freshets into a channel extending around the lake. When a deposit of sediment cannot be prevented, it can be cleaned out by various methods. It is usually rich in plant-food and might be useful in improving poor land or in preparation for planting trees. For this purpose, the deposit can be obtained by using a suction pump, or if the water can be drained off, by hauling the sediment away in carts or cars. If not needed, the sediment can be washed into the stream below by opening a gate in the dam.

For good appearance and for economy in construction, lakes should be located in ravines, valleys or depressions. One advantage in forming a lake by damming a stream and filling its valley with water is that the shores of such a lake, especially along its sides where the water is confined

by natural slopes of the valley, will usually be
satisfactory in outline. The dam will be the difficult part to manage. The site for this should be
chosen where the valley is narrow. Ample provision must be made in the overflow for the largest freshet that can come. The water in falling
over the dam would gouge out any yielding material.
A durable cement apron must, therefore, be constructed with protection at the sides, and this must
be carried to a point where the flow of the stream
below the dam is comparatively level. It is well
to subordinate this cement apron by inserting
bowlders while the cement is soft and by making
use also of cobblestones, gravel and overhanging
bushes. If the overflow can be prolonged into a
series of falls and rapids with intervening pools,
it will add interest to the lake's outlet and aid in
producing a natural effect. No masonry or cement
work should rest on filled ground. If the overflow
is carried along the side of the valley instead of
the center for a short distance it may help in getting
a solid foundation, and in giving an interesting variation to the line of the channel. When the valley
in which the dam is constructed is broader than the
space required for the greatest overflow, a portion

of the dam may be an earth embankment which should be carried well above high-water mark. In the center of this embankment a core wall should be constructed — not for strength, but to keep muskrats and other water animals from burrowing through. A thin wall will answer the purpose, but it should be carried well into the bank on either side. It need not extend above high water in the lake. If the earth embankment is broadened where it joins the natural bank, and planted in harmony with the growth along the sides of the lake, it will aid in giving a natural appearance. Earth embankments, even when built of sand and gravel, may be made water-tight by mixing clay in the stream which they obstruct, the sand filtering out the clay from the water flowing through the embankment until all interstices are closed. The bottom of artificial lakes may be made tight by a layer of puddled clay. If a sand or gravel bottom is desired, these materials can be placed on top of this waterproof layer.

There are advantages and disadvantages in stocking a lake with fish. If the water is cold enough, trout and bass would be unobjectionable. Carp, while keeping the water free from certain objectionable weeds, usually stir up the bottom so that the water becomes muddy. This is also true of goldfish. Mosquitoes in the larva state (wigglers) are eaten by fish. A lake which is large enough to be stirred by the wind will be free from wigglers except where the water is kept stationary by cattails or other water-loving plants. Mosquitoes are sometimes killed by the application of kerosene or other oils to the surface of the water. A lake has so many attractions that one can afford to take some trouble to keep it free from weeds and mosquitoes.

To insure a lake's appearing at its best, the banks should be low at those points of the shore over which the water is most frequently observed (Fig. 23). Thus, borders nearest a veranda or the windows of a house from which the lake is seen should be low so that the surface of the water will be visible its entire length in the line of view. On the other hand, banks which are seen meeting the water each side of a view may be steep and high and covered with a high growth. A list of plants suitable for covering the low borders would include Virginia creepers and other vines, violets, marsh marigolds, certain kinds of iris, grass of Parnassus, bluets, forget-

I

me-nots, white clover, ground ivy, and many others.

The high banks which are glimpsed across the water, but which do not lie between any principal point of view and the lake, offer good opportunities

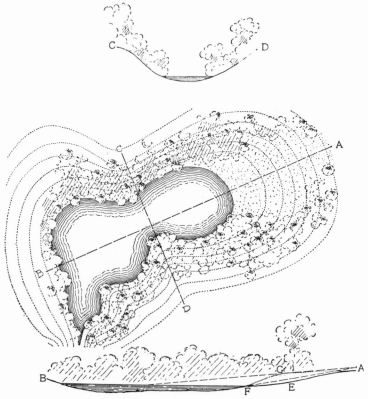

FIG. 23. — A LANDSCAPE LAKE. Showing plan and sections of artificial lake and its surroundings. Section *A B* shows point of site *A*. With grade as shown by full line *A E F*, the entire length of the lake is seen. With grade shown by dotted line *A G F*, a large portion of the lake is hidden.

for attractive groupings of trees and shrubs. On a south bank, a mixture of hemlocks and birches would be pleasing, with a ground covering of yews and ferns in certain places. On the sunny north slopes, if one desired rich autumn coloring, one could not do better than to select sugar maples anywhere in the northern portion of the eastern half of the United States. Other trees noted for their fall coloring, but found in a more restricted area, include sassafras, tulip trees, birches, white ash, sweet gum, flowering dogwood, pepperidge, blue beech, pin cherries, and some of the oaks. The staghorn sumac, which often grows to the size of a small tree, is rich in color and so are all the other sumacs. The shrubby dogwoods turn purple, red, and yellow. The common hazel is often wonderful in color. Other maples help to make American autumns glorious, the red maple being especially brilliant in certain portions of New England, where it is frequently accompanied by the equally brilliant blueberry. All of the above native trees are suitable for planting about artificial lakes when these are extensive enough to provide space along their borders for both openings and woods.

Islands may furnish additional space for planting. When these are introduced, they should be so placed as not to diminish the apparent size of the lake. They would naturally be located relatively near one of the shores. They hide a portion of the lake and thus help to make it interesting. They also furnish an excellent opportunity to show marginal planting to advantage.

When one thinks of New England, certain portions of the middle states, and the region traversed by the Alleghany mountains, other plants come to mind which should certainly be mentioned in the abbreviated list given here as suitable for planting about lakes. These are the rhododendrons, azaleas, mountain laurels, sweet pepper bushes, bayberries, andromedas, wild roses and hollies, including the inkberry and the winterberry. The spring-flowering plants of woody growth would include, besides many of those already mentioned, the juneberry, red-bud, crab-apples and thorn-apples, elderberries, and many others. If there are open areas stretching away from a lake, one can imagine them covered with herbaceous plants which may flower from spring until fall. If the ground in such an area is quite moist, the sequence of bloom might include marsh marigolds, iris, marsh-mallows, lilies, various eupatoriums, including Joe-Pye weed, some species of helianthus, ironweed, lobelias, snakeheads, ladies' tresses, gentians, asters, and grass of Parnassus. If the banks of a lake are steep and somewhat gravelly or rocky, columbines, saxifrages, harebells, butterfly-weeds, goldenrods, and some of the asters would be at home. On steep banks that are moist and shady, one would expect to find trilliums, hepaticas, wild ginger, adder-tongues, bloodroots, squirrel-corn, maidenhair ferns, mosses and liverworts.

If a lake is near a house or in a city square, it would be allowable to plant the more usual forms of cultivated plants about its borders, but when the graceful wild beauty of a natural lake is desired, one would not expect to see such subjects as lilacs and peonies.

The designing of artificial lakes, embracing, as it should, some knowledge of engineering, a study of outlines, ability in grading and a wide acquaint-ance with plants, requires great skill in the art of landscape-gardening and furnishes a good test of the designer's proficiency.

CHAPTER VIII

Home Grounds

Thus far, this book has taken up mainly general principles and a study of those features that might be introduced into any ornamental grounds. It will now discuss the application of those principles to the development of grounds for special purposes. The devotion of land to home grounds may very properly be considered first, since such grounds are so widely distributed, have existed for such a long time, and are so intimately connected with all lives; for even if a man lives in an apartment building or a hotel, he has friends whose home grounds he enjoys, or he hopes to have grounds of his own sometime.

When one considers the development of grounds for special purposes, one must first have clearly in mind what these objects are. What purposes are served by home grounds? They are often called private grounds, and this indicates one service they may render. There are many others.

The house gives protection from weather, a place where one may regulate the temperature, read, play, eat, and sleep. Its windows also provide views of the outside world and allow sunshine and air to enter. It is largely through them that the work of the architect is connected with that of the landscape-gardener. The latter must realize : first, that the persons who live in the house and their guests need sunlight, air, and an attractive outlook when they are in the house; second, that the approach to the house should be easy and natural; third, that impressions of the house and grounds from the usual outside points of view and especially from points along the approach drive or walk should be pleasing; fourth, that a reasonable degree of privacy should be enjoyed in the grounds as well as in and about the house; fifth, that special features like front lawns, flower-gardens, swimming-pools, vegetable-gardens, service yards, bird baths, summer-houses, seats, garages, stables and chicken-houses should be so placed as to be arranged conveniently with regard to each other and the purposes they are to serve and also appear well in the landscape or general composition of the home.

In making a home, the first proceeding after

choosing a lot is to select a site for the house. Remembering the value of sunshine in the living-rooms, the house will advisedly be well supplied with windows on the east, south, and west sides. It is from these windows that the grounds will be seen, and as these grounds should have an appearance of freedom and seem as extensive as conditions will allow, the house should usually be placed near the north line of the lot. Exceptions to this rule may be made, however, when there is a permanent open space adjoining the south line of the lot like that insured by a river, lake, park, valley or stretch of relatively low land. If the lot itself is low near the north boundary, and high along the south side, or if it has marked variations of level, or commands exceptionally fine views in any direction, these facts may lead to a modification of the rule given above. The site selected should be one that can be well drained, in fact, as well as have the appearance of being so. A house placed with reference to the conditions so far stated will usually but not always have the benefit of the most needed breezes (Fig. 24).

The direction of the prevailing winds should have due consideration. With a small lot, the main

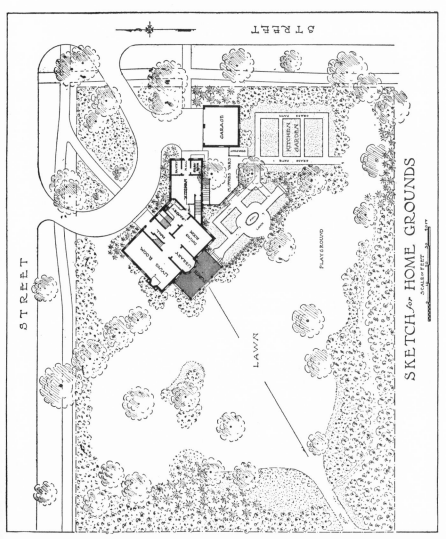

FIG. 24. — PLAN FOR HOME GROUNDS. The house is placed at angle with streets, enabling the living-rooms and porch to command best views and receive southwest breeze. Plan shows complete turnaround for automobiles, part of this turnaround being formed by street pavements.

lines of the house will preferably parallel the lot boundaries, but with ample room it may be wise to face the house with reference to topography, view, or breeze, instead of placing it with regard to the lines of the lot or street. Protection from the cold north or northwest winds may sometimes be sought and be secured partially by placing the house on a south or southeast slope, or by having a protecting belt of planting.

In most cases, the site for a house can be easily reached from the highway, and so the choice of its location is made with reference to other considerations. Occasionally, however, difficulty or ease of access may have more weight in determining the place for a house than even the view or some of the other factors which have been mentioned. If a drive is required, the house usually should be placed so there will be room for this drive between the house and north lot boundary, or between the house and the nearest boundary. If the drive and the entrance to which it leads can be on the side of the house not devoted to living-rooms and verandas or terraces, the latter will be free from intrusion (Fig. 25). This fact may also have a bearing on the house's location. Finally, existing trees or other

growth may influence the location of the house.
A great oak that has been growing a hundred years

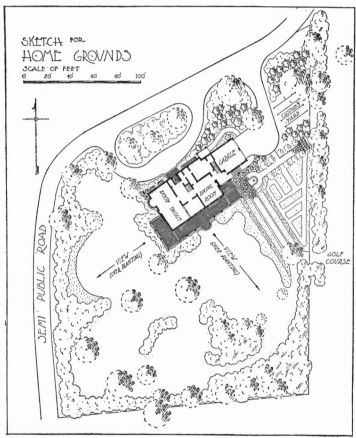

FIG. 25. — ANOTHER EXAMPLE. Sketch for home grounds in Winnetka, Ill.

may help to make a beautiful picture if it stands
in proper relation to the dwelling.   It is worth while

to make such a picture by selecting a house location with reference to such a tree. This would be true if in place of the oak there were any other desirable tree or group of trees, or a group of shrubs that could not easily be moved.

The method of reaching a house is the next step after the determination of its site. Three cases will be considered: (a) when only a walk is required; (b) when a drive answers also for a walk; (c) when the situation calls for both a walk and a drive.

(a) Walks should lead in an easy natural way from a point of beginning to a destination. When a walk is an approach to a house, its point of beginning is either the place where one leaves the street sidewalk or where one alights from an automobile. The destination will be the entrance door of the house or the steps leading to it. If this door faces the street and the distance is short, the walk may with propriety be straight. If the distance to be traveled is considerable and the lot large, a curved walk will usually fit the situation better, especially if the street approach is mostly from one direction. To determine the location of the curved walk, one should think of the lot as being graded and covered with a turf, but without any definite walk. The path that one would then naturally follow in going from office to entrance door would usually indicate the proper location for the permanent walk. This location, which would ordinarily be a graceful curve without reverses, might be modified to avoid a tree or cutting into the lawn in a disagreeable way. If the surface of the lot is varied, if there are hills, valleys, or ravines, the walk may wind back and forth to a limited extent to secure an easy grade, but a serpentine line should be used as little as possible. The most satisfactory curve is one in which the rate of curvature continually changes in one direction, that is, from a gentle curve to one more pronounced, or the reverse, instead of being uniform as in a circle.

The grade of a walk should be easy, preferably not more than one-half inch rise in one foot, although it is better to have a rise of one inch in a foot than to provide steps. The use of steps may lead to an uncomfortable jolt, or even a dangerous fall at night unless they are well lighted. Sometimes, however, steps are necessary, and then the rule of two risers and one tread equaling twenty-five inches is a good one when the riser is not less than three or four inches. If the grade is just in excess of that permitted for a walk, a riser of four to six inches with a tread requiring three footsteps from one step to the next is allowable, the odd number of footsteps being used to insure the lifting from one tread to the next being done alternately by the muscles of each leg (Fig. 26).

A width of five feet is suitable for most walks to private houses. A cross-section with a slight crown gives a better appearance than a flat surface. The material used may be concrete, brick, asphalt, or stone. Concrete is smooth and durable, but its light color is objectionable. This, however, may be modified by the introduction of coloring matter or by giving the surface a granular appearance with fine gravel. A brick walk is good in color, and if moss or other fine vegetation grows in the joints, it may be unusually pleasing.

Before the walk is laid, the ground should be drained. If the land is high on one side and low on the other, surface water from the former should be carried to the latter underneath the walk through a pipe or culvert with a good fall to some outlet,

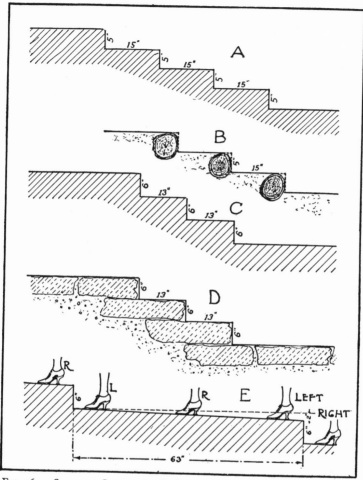

Fig. 26. — Showing Steps. A, C, Concrete steps illustrating the rule of 2 risers and 1 tread equaling 25 inches. B, Steps formed by using logs and backing with earth. D, Stone steps. E, Step with long tread.

which should be ample so that water will not stand in the pipe and freeze.

A good method of staking a walk is to carry on one arm a bundle of small stakes from one to three feet long and drop these one at a time along the route to be followed, spacing the stakes at uniform distances by pacing. An assistant will drive these stakes where they are dropped but only deep enough to secure them in a vertical position until they are lined to a satisfactory curve. To secure such a curve, one should look along the line of stakes, starting at one end, and direct the assistant to move each stake to the right or left until it is in the proper place. The entire line should be gone over in this way from each direction, repeating the lining if necessary, until the curve is satisfactory from any point of view. The uniform spacing of the stakes is advisable. Where a reverse is necessary, the stakes should gradually approach a straight line until the point of reverse is reached and then as gradually leave the straight line, the curve becoming more pronounced as one proceeds. While the curve approaches a straight line, it should never reach it; that is, the curve should be continuous from one end to the other without any "tangents" (Fig. 27).

Hardly any work is more interesting than staking a beautiful line. The line of stakes may be in the center or at one side of the proposed walk, and measurements can be taken from each stake at right angles to the line to determine the location of the "form" at the edge of the walk. The profile or line determining the grade or vertical position of

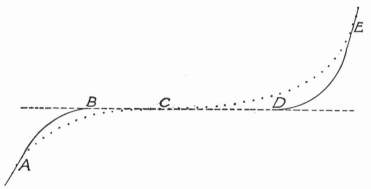

Fig. 27. — THE WALK. Dots show stakes for center line of road. This curve gradually approaches a straight line at point of reverse C. The continuous curve is better than arcs of circles with straight lines.

the walk may be fixed in much the same way by driving the stakes to a pleasing vertical curve. Instead of sighting over the tops of the stakes, it is more convenient to have three T's or rods of equal length, say four feet, and sight over the tops of these when they are held vertically resting on the tops of three consecutive stakes. Two assistants will be needed to hold these rods, the one

K

at the third stake being directed to drive it until the line over the tops of the rods is satisfactory. When the stake is driven to the proper grade, each assistant and the observer move forward along the line to the next stake and thus continue until all the stakes in the line are driven to the desired grade. When the profile of the grade is straight, the tops of the three T's will be in line. When it is convex upward, the third stake will be driven until the top of the T resting upon it is below the line over the tops of the other two, the distance below the line depending on the rate of vertical curvature. When the grade is concave upward, the third stake will be driven so that the T resting upon it will show above the line over the tops of the other two T's. By repeating the trials for grade in a way similar to that used in determining horizontal curves, a satisfactory profile can be found quickly. With a hand level, it is easy to determine when the grade is within proper limits.

It has been stated that when a walk is curved, the curve should continue from end to end. It is a mistake to introduce a complete circular walk inclosing a flower-bed, fountain, or statue, with the center of this circle in the center of the direct walk to the house (Fig. 28). If a tree or shrub which is good enough to be saved stands in the natural line of the walk, one should not make an abrupt détour around it, but shift the line for a long distance so that the curve will be good and leave the tree at one side.

The surface of the walk should meet at its edge the surface of the ground, the latter continuing for

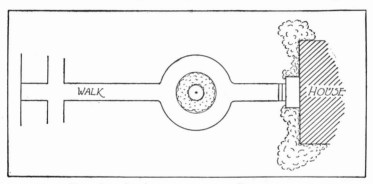

FIG. 28. — AN ARRANGEMENT NOT RECOMMENDED.

a short distance the slope of the former and then joining by a graceful curve the general grade of the land. This not only gives a good appearance, but it allows the water to run off from the walk. Some gardeners and janitors have a penchant for making a ditch along each edge of a walk. Such ditches are ugly in themselves even before they catch the papers and other refuse that will be swept into them.

With a little care, the lawn will meet the walk in a neat, sharp line, but it is far better to have a few blades of grass lie on the walk than to disfigure it with ditches.

(b) Much of what has been said regarding walks will apply to drives. If a lot is narrow, a straight drive from the street along the side of the house is proper. This may be used as a walk if it leads to the entrance door. If this door is in the front of the house facing the street, it may be reached by a short walk branching from the drive (Fig. 29). This arrangement saves expense and, what is more important, it provides an unbroken area between the street and the house to be developed into a thing of beauty. If the house is quite far from the highway, it is allowable to divert the entrance drive from a direct route somewhat for the sake of following the edge of a ravine or valley, passing a pond, tree, or other object of special interest, or bringing into notice one or more pleasing views, but the best view of all should be seen after entering the house and passing to the windows on the other side from the entrance. The immediate approach to the house on a slightly ascending grade is usually better than on either a level or descending grade.

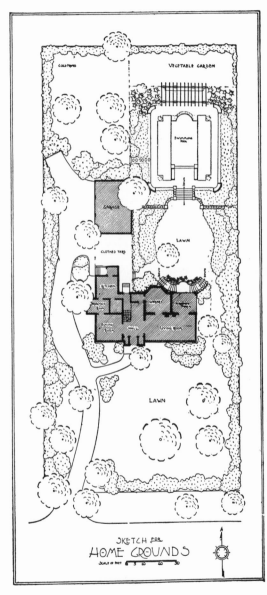

FIG. 29. — THE SETTING OF THE HOUSE. Sketch for home grounds, Cedar Rapids, Iowa.

It is desirable by the location of the drive and the arrangement of the planting to bring the house into view at a point where its appearance is most pleasing. From this point one will usually see two sides of the house and it will appear to be of the proper size.

With automobiles, a drive having a reasonably hard, even surface is required. Such a drive is well adapted for a walk, and on a private approach the number of vehicles passing will not be great enough materially to interfere with the comfort of walking. A combined walk and drive, or rather a drive which is also used for a walk, appears better than two passageways through the lawn and planting. Moreover, its cost for construction and maintenance will be less. This method of reaching the house will, therefore, be advisable in many, perhaps in most cases.

(c) Sometimes, however, to insure greater privacy or safety, to secure more varied effects, or to allow the approach to the house from different directions, one or more walks may be needed in addition to the drive (Fig. 30). The location and construction of each would be in accordance with principles and directions given under (a) and (b).

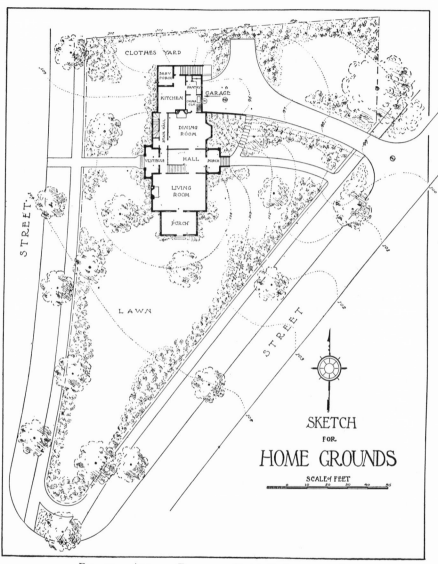

FIG. 30.—ANOTHER EXAMPLE. Sketch for home grounds,
Cedar Rapids, Iowa.

Complete directions for the construction of drives are not included in this book, since these are easily found in treatises on engineering or government bulletins. It is the desire here to emphasize the importance of their location for convenience, comfort, and good appearance. The laying out of a walk or drive on any desired grade is, however, so simple and generally useful that every one who has a farm or a large "place" in city or country should know how to do it. A hand level costing about six dollars is the only instrument required. With this, by merely sighting through, one can look in any direction and determine a horizontal line extending from the eye. To illustrate how a line on any desired grade is located, suppose the observer's eye, when he is standing, to be five feet from the ground, and the desired grade five per cent. Stand at a low point on the proposed line. With the level select a point that is of the same height as the eye on the higher ground ahead and about one hundred feet away. Have an assistant pace one hundred feet toward this point and then direct him to move to the right or left until the spot upon which he stands is just on a level with the cross wire of the instrument. He will mark

this spot and then pace forward to another spot
one hundred feet further on and five feet above the
first spot determined, while the observer moves
in like manner to the spot the assistant has just
marked. By repeating this process, a line can be
marked rising at the rate of five per cent. If the
line along the desired route should descend, the
observer will go ahead and sight back. If the line
goes around a rise of the land which hides the point
one hundred feet away, fifty feet can be paced instead of one hundred, and the observer will sight
to a point on the assistant's clothing two and one-
half feet above the ground on which he stands.
For greater accuracy, the assistant can use a rod
on which feet and fractions of a foot are plainly
marked, and the distance can be measured with a
tape, but for preliminary work, the method outlined is rapid and sufficiently accurate to determine whether the proposed line for a walk or drive
is feasible or not. If conditions are favorable, that
is, if the ground is open and reasonably smooth
so that pacing will show rather closely the actual
distance, the method outlined may answer for the
final determination of the proposed line. It will
also determine whether the grade must be changed.

If a six per cent grade is required, the assistant for the observer, whose eye is five feet above the ground, would pace eighty-three and one-third feet instead of one hundred. For an easier grade, the assistant would pace farther when on an ascending grade and the observer would do the pacing on a descending grade. If the observer's eye was more than five feet above the ground, the distance paced would be correspondingly greater.

For a large place, there will be many walks or drives in addition to those approaching the house from the highway, especially if there is uneven ground or forest, and the location of such walks and drives will be determined by methods similar to those just described.

Having selected the site for the house and the location of the approaches to it from the highway, the landscape-gardener will proceed to choose sites for the other features desired by his client. These sites will be discussed briefly, approximately in the order of their importance.

GARAGES

Nearly everyone who builds a house will require a garage. There are many positions which it may occupy. It should be subordinated to the house. It is well, although not absolutely essential, for it not to be visible at all on the approach to the house. Sometimes it is even advisable to place it on the street or between the street and the house at one side of the drive. It may form a part of the house. Occasionally, when the topography is favorable, it may be placed in the basement. Sometimes it may be in an extension of the kitchen wing, or separated from the kitchen by a service yard. Again it will be at a distance, hidden from the house, where all noise connected with cleaning and repairing cars will be out of hearing, or it may be on an entirely different lot and perhaps a block or more away from the residence. The wishes of the owner will be the determining factor in its location, but the landscape-gardener should be able to suggest the most favorable positions, and when the site is chosen, arrange planting so as to give the best possible effect. Usually in front of the garage there must be space for turning. This space should be bounded at least partially by curved lines with radii of not less than twenty feet. It is assumed that a car will need a circle sixty feet in diameter in which to turn, but since it can turn by backing and then going ahead, a full circle is not always required. It is important to have room enough for comfort, also to make the garage as unobtrusive as possible.

SERVICE YARDS

Service yards naturally will be placed where they will be easily accessible from the kitchen and laundry. Like garages, they should be unobtrusive. A service yard furnishes a place for drying clothes, for storing temporarily supplies for the kitchen, and sometimes as a place of recreation for the servants. It should be at the end or back of the kitchen wing and may be inclosed by a wall, a fence, or a hedge of shrubbery. There would be no objection to planting trees north of a service yard, but they should not be placed where they will shade the yard during drying hours. When shrubs are used to give the desirable seclusion, they may appear as a natural group on the outside, and be trimmed for convenience along the boundaries of the service yard. Two shrubs most suitable for use in this connection are lilac and syringa (Philadelphus), as they have many branches and make a screen even in winter. Evergreens, when hardy, will perhaps make a better screen than any deciduous shrub, but, in most cities, they are unreliable on account of the smoke. If evergreens can be used, arbor-vitae and hemlocks are good because they can be kept from growing too high. Broad-leaved evergreens are suitable wherever they are hardy and attain sufficient size. When walls or fences are used, they furnish a suitable place for vines. The south side of an inclosing wall is suitable for raising grapes, climbing roses, Virginia creepers and clematis. Nearly all vines are satisfactory, provided a wire netting is placed for those not self-attaching.

FRONT YARDS

While garages and service yards are a necessity, from one point of view they are less important than the front yard. Their relation to the latter is much like that of the kitchen to the living-room or library. The front yard, meaning the open space on which may face the living-room, library, dining-room and veranda or terrace, should be the most artistic part of the home grounds. From every viewpoint, it should appear beautiful enough to photograph or paint. A front yard

should have open space to show sky, clouds and
sunshine. The sky space is bounded preferably
by the outlines of trees and bushes. Such outlines, if the growth is allowed to be natural, are
sure to be graceful and pleasing. They will be high
at one spot and low in another. They will be near
at hand at one point and may be miles away in
another direction. Sometimes a sky-line may descend to the ground, perhaps touching a hill, a
prairie, or a range of mountains. If the hill is far
away, no jarring effect may be produced, but, if
close at hand, it is usually best to soften even the
outline of the hill with some foliage. Sometimes
the sky-line descends to a body of water which
stretches away to the horizon. In such cases, after
meeting its surface, the sky-line continues below the
water, which may occupy a position in the real
picture similar to that of the sky. This water,
which may be a lake, a sea, or an ocean, should
have its outline softened. If one looks out over a
closely shaven lawn at a body of water, the effect
is not as pleasing as when the edge of the lawn is
modified by an indefinite growth like that of vines,
bushes, or the graceful forms of certain herbaceous
plants.

The ground of the front yard may be covered with grass or creeping plants. Between it and the sky-line there will appear a bank of foliage. This bank may be steep, may even overhang, giving a deep shade, or it may have a very gradual slope tapering off toward a distant view. It may be formed entirely of one kind of growth, yet appear varied because of the different amounts of light received in various parts. The foliage in itself may be varied, the leaves of certain trees or shrubs being glossy, while that of others is dull. The leaves may show a thousand different shapes. The bank of foliage may be sprinkled with flowers or with fruits. The branches of trees or shrubs may spread far out over the ground in one place and recede in another out of sight. The boundary of trees and shrubs may be deciduous or evergreen. In the former case, a curtain or bank of trunks and branches will take the place of leaves in winter.

The winter effect may be exceedingly interesting, due to the various shades of color shown by the bark of twigs and trunks of trees, to the forms and colors of buds, and to the method of branching. With the leaves gone, the sky-line drops to a lower level, the space between its summer and winter positions being filled with an open, lace-like tracery against a light background. At times this background is white, and the network of branches against it is more beautiful than the finest etching. Again, the lace-work of branches may be seen against a brilliant evening sky of red or yellow and give the impression of far deeper coloring than when such a sky is observed entirely in the open.

Occasionally, it may be interesting to have an opening through the bank of foliage or boughs, this opening being entirely surrounded with growth and framing a distant landscape. Such an opening, however, must be studied with care and placed so it will not lessen the charm of the front yard itself. Perhaps it would be best to keep the opening through the trees invisible from the house and let it come as a pleasant surprise from some bay or path where a seat might be placed.

The kinds of trees and shrubs that should be selected to form the front yard boundary will depend on the size of the yard, the lie of the land, the views to be kept open, the soil and the climate. Preference usually should be given to existing growth. An oak tree that has been growing for a large part of a century is very likely to fit the local conditions, and if these are not changed by the removal of a natural mulch of leaves, the lowering of the water-table, or in some other way, the tree should live for another hundred years. A study of the native woods in the vicinity will help materially in solving the problem of what to plant. As it is important not to cut off sunshine from the house, a small place should not have tall-growing trees, especially toward the east, south and west, when the lines of the rooms are parallel to the cardinal points of the compass. Sometimes a large tree may be placed diagonally out from the corner of the house and do no harm, because the sun can shine directly into all the rooms at some time during the day. A personal fondness for certain plants will play a large part in the selection. Some persons like lilacs and others do not. Some have an aversion to evergreens, and others wish them in abundance. In making the choice, one is determining what to place against the sky canvas. One is selecting the forms and colors that harmonize with each other at all seasons of the year and especially during the time the house is to be occupied. The choice of plants may be influenced by one's preference for etchings or paintings.

M

The joining of the boundary growth with the lawn or ground cover calls for the exercise of skill. Satisfactory effects may result from allowing the lower branches of trees to spread out in their search for light and rest upon the lawn. Certain shrubs, like aromatic sumac, are well adapted for the border of an open space, as their lower branches spread horizontally, thus giving a graceful receding outline. In a shadowy bay with more upright growth, a bed of ferns may find a congenial home. There are many flowering plants which like some shade and will help to make the front yard beautiful when they are planted near its south boundary. For the flowers which like sunshine, appropriate places can be found along the north side of open areas. A continuous uniform border of flowers, however, along the margin of groups of shrubs does not look well. One's aim should be to introduce trees, shrubs and flowers that will give harmonious combinations of color, effective contrasts of light and shade and graceful pleasing outlines.

The floor of the front yard, the area about a house usually covered with turf, may be treated in various ways. Its grade must first be determined. The house should appear to be on the highest land in its immediate vicinity. Even when placed on a hillside, there should be a narrow valley between the foundation of the house and the hill for appearance as well as for surface drainage. If the ground selected for a house site is level, its appearance will be greatly improved by even a slight variation from a flat surface. Usually the earth excavated for foundations and basement or cellar can be

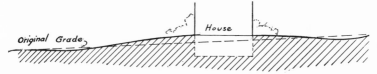

FIG. 31. — THE SURFACE LINES. Showing grades about house.

employed to make a broad gentle mound where the house is to stand (Fig. 31). Sometimes additional emphasis may be given to the mound by depressing the natural level surface beyond or outside of the fill about the house. Sometimes, if the grounds are extensive, it may even be wise to make a hill in one place and a valley in another. In determining the grade, there is a chance for the exercise of considerable ingenuity, but the final result must appear natural and dignified, not childish or artificial.

The first step in the actual building of a house, perhaps after the construction of a road, should be the removal of all the good top soil from the site of the house and those portions of its surroundings which would be covered in the final grade. This soil should be put in one or more piles out of the way of building operations, yet conveniently near so that it can be easily replaced about the house after its completion. The lines of the finished grade should flow naturally into each other in every direction without sharp angles. Projecting rock ledges or bowlders are unobjectionable. They often make the grounds more beautiful and sometimes furnish admirable places for ferns, vines, mosses, lichens, or other plants. When the grading is done, the usual procedure is to sow lawn seed. There is hardly anything more beautiful than a well-kept, gently rolling lawn. The dew upon it in the morning, the play of sunlight on it, and its yielding to the pressure of one's foot, are delightful. Yet it is sometimes advisable to use other plants than grass and white clover for a ground cover. To mention but a few, one might list trailing juniper, horizontal cotoneaster, bearberry, spurge, partridge-berry, the low forms of yew, myrtle, violets, Virginia creeper, wild grapes, lily-of-the-valley, virgin's bower, wintergreen, wandering Jew, iris, and day lily. The opportunities for experimenting in this direction are unlimited.

Having secured a satisfactory ground cover for the open area, one must join this agreeably with the walls of the house or terrace. Sometimes this is done for two or three months with a certain measure of success by using such plants as cannas, geraniums or begonias, but for the year round, plants with a hardy woody growth must be chosen, usually shrubs or vines. The height of the plantation about the house can be varied as is the sky-line opposite. It can drop to the ground in places to give light to low windows or show some architectural feature of the house, and climb to the roof in others. The shrubs selected may spread out away from the house or grow to a height sufficient to screen a veranda from the street. They may be chosen for beauty of leaves, blossoms, berries, for perfume or for color of twigs. The features of a front yard, the open space, the ground cover below, and the border plantations, may be common to all home grounds whether large or small. Even with the smallest grounds, there is opportunity for endless enjoyment in planting interesting and beautiful things, in watching them grow, smelling their perfume, guiding the growth of their general effect by adding in one place or taking away in another.

And what of the final result, the completed front yard? There never is any final result. The front yard is a continual growth, which may be so beautiful as to fill its owner with a constant desire to return to it whenever he is away; a place not only beautiful but restful because of its freedom from intrusion and its quietness and also because it is a part of its owner — is in fact his Garden of Eden. It is the most perfect example of the landscape-gardener's art, but while the landscape-gardener may make the original design, in its most perfect form it must be developed, adopted and loved by its owner. Into it will come birds with song, beautiful in shape and color and graceful in movement. Into it will come snow, rain, and sunshine. Into it will come the owner and his friends to enjoy their hours of leisure and from it they will watch the sun, moon, stars, the clear blue sky, clouds, and rainbows.

There are some persons, perhaps many, who will not appreciate this expression of the landscape-gardener's art. To them sky-lines, the winter with

its bare branches, and the summer with its green
foliage, make no appeal. A similar statement might
be made with regard to the work of painters and
musicians, yet a knowledge and appreciation of
painting and music add greatly to one's comfort
and enjoyment in life, and so would a knowledge
of landscape-gardening and an appreciation of the
beauty of nature. The landscape-gardener can do
no more useful thing for his client than to teach
him to see this beauty, since, by so doing, he will
give him more pleasure in living during the entire
remaining portion of his life. The space which
has been called "the front yard" and which may
lie on at least three sides of a house is especially
adapted to show natural beauty because it is seen
so constantly. "Front yard" may not be the best
term to apply to this space. It has been called
the owner's Garden of Eden, and it is a garden in its
best sense, yet to use the term "garden" might
bring to mind a vegetable- or flower-garden, features
which should ordinarily be kept out of the front
yard. This yard may indeed have many flowers,
but these blossoms should come naturally like those
on a hawthorn, crab-apple, lilac, or in a peony or
iris bed. Such flowers do not interfere with the

feeling of repose that should exist in the front yard. To insure this feeling, the public street should, in a large measure, be excluded from view, especially that part nearest the house. It has sometimes been said that a home owner should not be selfish, that he should allow the public to see his beautiful grounds. In answer to this, it may be said that for the public a glimpse into such grounds, a glimpse leading to the exercise of one's imagination, is far more interesting than to have the property entirely exposed to view. Such glimpses can be provided without destroying privacy.

In many cases, the walk to the front door may lie within the front yard and be bordered with flowers. Another allowable feature is a bird bath, provided this is unobtrusive and conveniently placed beneath the branches of a tree, or near a group of shrubs where birds can preen their feathers after bathing. A sun-dial on the north side of a front yard, or perhaps on a terrace, or the south wall of the house, is unobjectionable, but it should not stand in the middle of a lawn.

With smaller houses, the dining-room and living-room may be united into one, and if a house is quite small, even the kitchen may be included in this one room. In like manner, a small yard may comprise more features than should be contained in a large one. For the sake of retaining the largest available space about a house, a small yard may even include the flower- and kitchen-gardens, and occasionally the service yard as well. In describing the front yard, the aim has been to call to mind what is ideal, an arrangement of grounds and planting that will give most pleasure to the intelligent and appreciative.

FLOWER-GARDENS

When one thinks of the best, one often uses in connection with it the word flower, as the flower of manhood, the flower of the army, the flower of youth. Perhaps something of the same idea is present when one thinks of the most charming part of a plant. Many delightful books have been written about flower-gardens, and it would seem that the designing of such gardens ought to be a profession by itself. There might be designers for different kinds of gardens, one making a specialty of formal gardens, another of bog-gardens, and so on through the list, including gardens of special flowers like roses, peonies, chrysanthemums, and iris ; or special colors, as blue and white, or blue and yellow ; or special localities, as alpine gardens and rock-gardens ; or special positions, as wall-gardens and terrace-gardens ; or of a special time of the year, as a spring-garden or winter-garden. As there are books treating of almost every kind of garden and giving details of kinds of flowers and methods of cultivation, the flower-garden here will be considered only in its relations to other features of the home grounds.

While there should be flowers in the front yard, the flower-garden proper, devoted entirely to the raising of plants which are conspicuous or note-worthy for their bloom, should occupy a somewhat less commanding position. It might perhaps be seen with advantage from the end of a terrace or veranda or from one of the rooms of the house, but when the grounds have sufficient size, the flower-garden should be subordinate to the front yard. Sometimes it might with advantage be separated entirely from the house and reached only by a path which could be made an interesting feature by covering it with vines carried on suitable sup-ports or bordering it with special plants. A flower-garden may be planned as an attractive feature in

itself to be seen out-doors, or it may be for the
purpose of raising cut-flowers for table or house
decoration. It is well if it can become the pet or
hobby of one of the members of the household. One
may make a specialty of hardy chrysanthemums,
of peonies, gladioli and dahlias or wild flowers.
Ordinarily a flower-garden will be near the vegetable-garden for convenience in cultivation, the
two being taken care of by the same men. With
limited ground, the stable and chicken yard, if these
exist, will not be far away. There may be a separate
garden for roses. This should be reached conveniently from the house, but as it has much bare
ground and is for cut-flowers mainly, it should
not form a prominent feature of the landscape. Wild-
gardens, being usually a natural arrangement of
native flowers with graceful lines and cloud-like
shapes, may very properly appear here and there
in the front yard. They may intermingle with the
shrubbery or cover the ground under trees or fill
a meadow-like area. If the home grounds are
large enough for woods, the wild flower-garden
may be in a natural opening in these woods or may
indeed pervade their whole extent, forming a beautiful ground cover, especially in early spring.

Happily, in designing flower-gardens and other landscape work, there is more freedom than exists in architecture, and one may take advantage of any charming feature pertaining to the lands selected for a home. Some persons believe that because one builds an Italian house, there should be an Italian garden, forgetting the dissimilarity of climate, soil, and topography, and the impossibility of raising cypresses and other plants found in the formal gardens of Italy, or even plants resembling them. There is more reason for imitating a colonial garden, because the climate and soil in this country now are substantially the same that they were one or two hundred years ago. There is a fascination in the flowers that our grandmothers raised, aside from their intrinsic beauty. Still there have been changes which would naturally lead to variation in gardens and home grounds. When the country was new, it was nearly all covered with woods, and an opening covered partly with a velvety lawn and planted with the flowers that had been brought from England, Holland, France, Germany, and Sweden seemed the most attractive of home surroundings. Now that the woods have largely disappeared from those regions where there is most home building, the native growth is more appreciated. Nothing in nature is more charming than woods, delightful for children to visit and interesting even to older people. One should have this charm in intimate relationship with one's home, having woods when possible as a boundary of the front yard, or a background for the flower-garden. A copse or spur from the edge of woods might even extend toward the house to separate the front yard from the garden, and lengthwise through the center of this copse a path might lead to the wood boundary and with an opening to the flower-garden.

VEGETABLE-GARDENS

In city and suburban homes, vegetable-gardens can very properly be introduced for two purposes : one, to give pleasure to owners who might take delight in seeing lettuce, strawberries, peas, parsley, onions, beets, carrots, and other vegetables growing, just as they would in looking at a flower-garden; the other, the pleasure of having fresh vegetables which are far better than those which have lain in a grocery one or two days. Vegetables which are purchased are usually far cheaper than those which are raised, but they are not as good unless they can be bought directly from a gardener within an hour or two of the time they are gathered. If one takes care of his own garden, there would be compensation in the exercise and good health. One would also have the keen and justifiable satisfaction that comes from producing or raising things with one's own hands.

There are advantages in having the vegetables and flower-gardens near each other. The barn and chicken-house may be close at hand, but preferably not seen from the house. This will make it convenient for supplying the gardens with manure and other fertilizers, and tools can be kept in one of the buildings. Fruit-trees and small-fruits can be raised in connection with the garden. Fruit-trees and nut-trees are beautiful and may sometimes be combined with other trees to give a picturesque effect; or if the grounds are small, two or three apple or nut-trees might be all that would be needed for shade. Raspberries, on account of the color of the bark, are sometimes used for winter decoration the same as red-branched dogwoods or Carolina roses. Even vegetables may sometimes be employed for decoration, especially in very small places where the entire ground might be devoted to vegetables and flowers.

TERRACES

It has sometimes been stated that the architectural lines of the house should be carried out a certain distance by the straight lines of terraces, balustrades, and trimmed hedges. A terrace is really a part of a house and should be designed and built by the architect. If, however, the landscape-gardener is called into consultation with the owner and architect, as he should be, there are several questions to be considered: (a) Will the terrace be useful and serve a purpose which would not be cared for equally well by the ground? (b) Will the terrace cut off a view of a valley, hillside, or other attractive feature of the landscape as seen from the windows of the room or rooms facing the proposed terrace? (c) Will a terrace improve the appearance of the house as seen from the usual viewpoints?

(a) The usefulness of a terrace will depend somewhat on the climate, the time of day it would be frequented, the side of the house on which it is placed, and the habits of the family. Normally a terrace is a place to walk or sit in the open air. It is an outdoor extension of the rooms facing on it, and so would be useful when there are large gatherings. It may serve also as a place on which to exhibit special plants, generally those which are not hardy and must be kept in a greenhouse or a conservatory during the winter. A terrace is usually a favorable spot from which to observe the landscape and, if it were shaded from the afternoon sun, might in summer serve all the purposes of a living-room. If a house is located upon a side hill a terrace may very properly be carried out from the end of the building when its length is parallel to the contours of the hill. In this situation a terrace would give room for comfortable circulation which would not be provided by the ground itself. When, however, the ground is nearly level and the house is set low, there may be no occasion for building any terrace.

(b) If the house is on a side hill and located as suggested in (a), a terrace at its side would very likely cut off the view of the valley below, which would be of far more interest than the terrace itself to the persons looking from the windows.

(c) Occasionally a terrace may give to a house better proportions. Care should be taken, however, to avoid cutting off a view of the house as seen from a point far below. When a terrace would obstruct a view of the valley as seen from the dwelling, it would also cut off a portion of the house when seen from the valley. A broad terrace often gives to a house the appearance of standing on depressed land when the viewpoint is below the level of the terrace.

HEDGES

Trimmed hedges are not as pleasing in appearance as those having natural outlines, but sometimes they are necessary, as an untrimmed hedge would become too high. If the plants used for a hedge have interesting blossoms or fruit, these are usually cut off or prevented from developing when the hedge is trimmed. In some instances, it is allowable for a trimmed hedge to take the place of a balustrade.

HOUSE SURROUNDINGS

The fear that some persons have of bringing natural beauty, that is, the beauty of untrimmed trees and bushes, of natural slopes, ravines, streams, and lakes, near a house, would seem to be groundless, since there can be no more objection to having a window-frame inclose a beautiful picture which

M

the objects named would make, than there is to having a similar picture hung on the wall of a room. It is often possible to improve the appearance of a house as it is seen from a distance by planting so as to correct its proportions, soften its lines or hide those parts which ought not to be seen. There is hardly any building so beautiful that it cannot be improved by planting so as to leave something to the imagination.

WOODS

In what has already been said regarding home grounds, some mention has been made of woods, but this feature has not been emphasized sufficiently. On city lots and grounds of moderate size in any location, it will hardly be possible to have a bit of forest, since the open sky with sunshine is more valuable than a collection of trees, but even in such locations a thicket which has most of the characteristics of woods on a small scale might be introduced.

To illustrate, a lot having a width of one hundred feet, or perhaps less, might have in one corner a thicket with red-buds at the back, then hawthorns and perhaps a black haw or an elderberry (Fig. 32).

Underneath this the leaves might be allowed to remain and protect wild flowers, like anemones, erythroniums, trilliums, and bloodroots. A thicket of this kind would, for the most part, take care of

Fig. 32. — The Winter Landscape. A view from a library window looking into woods which might extend indefinitely, but in reality are not over one hundred feet in depth.

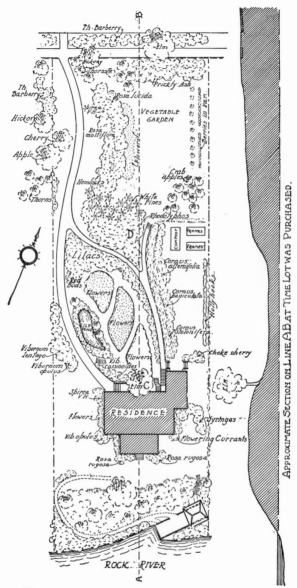

The labels within the figure:

Th. Barberry
Elm
Hickory
Thorns
Prickly Ash
Th. Barberry
Rosa lucida
Hickory
Spirea V.H.
VEGETABLE GARDEN
Cherry
Rosa multiflora
Apple
Hemlocks
Crab apples
Thorns
White Pines
Rhodotyphos
Berries to Jam
Frames
Frames
Corn
Lilacs
D
Cornus alternifolia
Red Buds
Flowers
Cornus paniculata
Flowers
Flowers
Cornus stolonifera
Viburnum lentago
Flowers
Choke cherry
Viburnum opulus
Vib. cassinoides
Hollyhocks
Spirea V.H.
Elm C
Flowers
RESIDENCE
Syringas
Vib. opulus
Flowering Currants
Rosa rugosa
Rosa rugosa
Rosa rugosa
ROCK RIVER

APPROXIMATE SECTION ON LINE AB AT TIME LOT WAS PURCHASED.

Fig. 33. — The Layout of a Private Place. With Figs. 34 to 40, it illustrates the development of a place of medium size. Lot is 100 feet wide by approximately 300 feet in length and lies between a street and Rock River at Dixon, Illinois.

itself, and with grounds of larger size the thicket
might be extended into a respectable forest through
which paths might lead to interesting objects.
America is rich in species of trees and shrubs and

Fig. 34. — In the Beginning. View from "D" on plan (Fig. 33), looking
toward river, 1909.

also in native flowers, and one who is developing an
American home ought certainly to make use of some
of the material close at hand, and thus develop a
restful retreat which might with propriety be called
"an American garden." (Figs. 33 to 40.)

FIG. 35. — To Start with. View from "C" on plan shown in Fig. 33, looking toward street at time lot was purchased, 1909.

FIG. 36. — The House in the Landscape. View showing relation of house to river.

FIG. 37. — AN UNIMPROVED PART OF THE LANDSCAPE. Valley used for potatoes in 1911. Natural growth of trees and bushes on bank preserved.

FIG. 38. — THE BUILDING STAGE. View of house just after completion in Fall of 1914. Elm tree preserved.

FIG. 39. — THE EFFECT OF PLANTING. House as seen from island in river. Note elm shown in second photograph.

A retreat of this kind will give its owner and his friends endless diversion and entertainment. It will also increase his interest in all that vegetation which comes of itself along roadsides, margins of woods and

FIG. 40. — THE OFFSCAPE. View from house to Rock River.

streams and other out-of-the-way places. It is this awakening of our senses to the beauty that exists wherever nature is given an opportunity to show her charms that will add zest to life, give individuality to one's home, and a value to grounds far beyond that which they may have in money.

CHAPTER IX

FARMS

THE importance of farms in the life of the country entitles them to a separate chapter, even though they are usually but one variety of home grounds. Farms might be thought of as the cradle of the nation. The farms do more for the cities than to furnish them food. They supply people for the cities as well. Since the average city family does not last through more than three or four generations, the population of a city must be replenished continually from the country. On this account, not only does the food supply of the nation depend on the farms but also its stability and character to a very large degree. The most influential citizens usually live in cities, but they or their antecedents came from the country. Our strong men owe their strength and ruggedness of character to the farms from which they sprang, and to these farms they often wish to return in their old age.

These facts have been mentioned to show the importance of the farm life in that of the nation as a whole, and the great benefit that may result from any improvement in the appearance, comfort and convenience of this feature of national life. It is very important, therefore, to consider the farm from a landscape-gardening point of view. With the good roads that are developing and with automobiles, auto-trucks and telephones, the social status of the farm will be greatly improved. Indeed the farmer, living where he can have good air to breathe and beautiful scenery to look at, may become the aristocrat (using the word in its best sense) [1] of the future.

Some of the questions to be considered on the farm and matters that will bring about improved conditions are here briefly discussed.

Where should the house be placed? The answer would be based on three considerations, namely, convenience, comfort, and appearance. For convenience, a house should sometimes be situated near the highway, but this is not always true. There are cases in which a more central location is desirable

[1] " Aristocrats are everywhere, they may have titles or they may have none. They are those who think they owe their best to God and men and they serve."
                                        PRICE COLLIER.

on account of the ease with which different parts of the farm may be reached from it. This would often be true of a dairy farm where the cows during a series of years would go from the barn, which would be conveniently near the house, to every field for pasture. A central location requires only short lanes to different fields and would save time in hauling hay and other crops to the storage place. The location of the water supply would have a bearing on the decision as to the building site.

The demands of comfort call for protection from cold winds in winter, the benefit of cooling breezes in summer, and sometimes more seclusion than accompanies a location near the highway. The shade of trees is also desirable to mitigate the heat of July and August. The site should have good drainage for air as well as for water.

For appearance, the site of the house should usually be on relatively high land. It should command good views and be favorably situated with regard to existing trees or other growth of value. On the farm a house can usually be placed without much regard to the street or boundary lines, that is, the important room or rooms can face a favorable breeze or view.

What planting should be done? If there are no trees about the site which is otherwise favorable for the house, trees can be planted. The list from which to choose would include all native forest trees as well as those introduced from other countries. Nut- and fruit-trees as well as the usual ornamental subjects are quite appropriate for planting about a group of farm buildings.

Before considering the planting, a plan for the various farm buildings should be made in which these are placed conveniently and picturesquely with regard to each other. The barn and other structures should be near the house for convenience, yet far enough away so that the noise of the animals and fowls will not be disturbing. The house should occupy a commanding position with regard to the other buildings and the farm itself. Care should be taken to place the barn, the chicken-house and other equipment where they will not cut off from the house a desirable breeze or view. When the buildings have been planned with regard to each other and also with due reference to farm operations, a planting scheme can be made. The suggestions in the preceding chapter are just as applicable to a farmer's home as to a city or suburban home. The object in planting should always be to make the surroundings beautiful. The farmer and his family need a "front yard," a piece of ground covered with restful turf and surrounded with trees far enough apart to give views of the surrounding country. A farmer's wife and daughters will receive as much enjoyment from a rose-garden or an old-fashioned flower-garden as would their city cousins. The barn-yard, the flower-garden, the chicken yard, the clothes yard, and other features may be separated from each other by lilacs and other old-fashioned shrubs. Evergreens also may be planted, perhaps more than will ultimately be needed, the surplus being either sold or used from time to time as Christmas trees.

An up-to-date farm will have a good supply of water under pressure and a little of this should be used for a bird-bath, or preferably for several such baths, which can be placed near trees or bushes where the birds can preen their feathers.

The re-stating of a few rules for planting will be in place here:

(1) Arrange the planting so that an ample supply of sunshine will reach the windows of the house.

(2) Plant so that the other buildings will be at least partially hidden from the house.

(3) Arrange the trees so that the best views will be preserved and framed.

(4) Plant trees and shrubs that are pleasing in themselves on account of their branches, blossoms, foliage or fruits and arrange them in irregular, graceful, harmonious groups.

(5) Plant shrubs to make a setting for the house. The shrubs selected will depend on the height of the window sills, the exposure, — that is whether on the east, west, north or south side of the house, — and the personal taste of those responsible for the plan.

(6) Introduce hardy perennials where they will have a good background and will thrive, but do not put flowers in the central part of the front yard.

(7) Do not plant deeper than plants stood in the place from which they were moved. This applies especially to trees and shrubs.

(8) Cultivate newly planted material as one would a vegetable-garden from May to the last of August.

(9) If water becomes necessary, use water copiously so the ground will be soaked and then omit watering for one or two weeks. Rake or hoe the surface of

the ground that has been watered as soon as it dries.

(10) Plant evergreens in cloudy or drizzly weather. Evergreen roots should never be exposed to sunlight.

(11) Plants received from a nursery should be put in the ground as soon as possible after they are received. If they cannot be placed permanently when they arrive, heel them in for a few days.

(12) Learn to see beauty during all seasons of the year in the things that are planted.

(13) Mulching will protect fall planting and will serve partially as a substitute for cultivation.

(14) After trees and shrubs become established, do very little trimming, cutting only dead branches and those which interfere with walks or drives. Cut such branches at their junction with the trunk or with a larger branch.

THE FARM FOREST

The question will arise as to whether the farm should have a wood-lot and if so what it should contain and where it should be located. Foresters will reply that every farm should have a wood-lot for the wood and lumber that it will furnish. They will state that a wood-lot will often save a trip to town for a stick of timber, and will often make the farmer independent of coal strikes. Even though coal is obtainable, a fire-place for wood makes a house cheerful and every farmer should have one and cut a supply cf wood for it from his own land. In the regions of hilly land, as New York and New England, the wood-lot is a natural part of the farm.

A wood-lot is a desirable feature for the farm from the point of view of a landscape-gardener even more than from that of a forester (Fig. 41). An area of woods helps to

N

FIG. 41. — THE FOREST IN THE LANDSCAPE. A farm wood-lot.

vary the sky-line and make it interesting and beautiful. The woods themselves are charming at all seasons of the year. The beauty of the country usually includes that of many farms, and the various wood-lots belonging to different owners frame in the distant views to be seen from any house. Study the effect of areas of woods from car windows and think how monotonous would be the appearance of the country if these woods were removed. Note at the edge of a pasture a single great elm or a group of oaks underneath whose branches cows are resting during the heat of a summer day, a picture of comfort and utility as well as beauty.

That farmer is most fortunate who has a bit of original forest on his land; an area that has never been cleared and contains a variety of growth. Compare such an area in New York or Ohio with a prairie tree-claim where the tree plantation is made up entirely of soft maples or box elders. In the former, there will be sugar maples, beeches, oaks, sycamores, black walnuts, butternuts, lindens, ashes, tulip trees, hickories, elms, hawthorns, crab-apples, red-buds, dogwoods, sassafras and many others, a combination that gives interest to life, while the latter area covered with one short-lived tree has a deadly monotony.

In selecting trees for a wood-lot that must be planted, one should use many kinds, endeavoring to reproduce as far as possible all the interesting features of the natural forest, not forgetting the wild flowers. The entire lives of farmers' sons and daughters will be enriched and made happier if they have an acquaintance with the native growth that has been suggested above and with the birds and animals that would take refuge in this growth.

While called a "wood-lot," it need not be a square or regular shaped area. It might stretch along a highway to which it will add comfort and attractiveness as well as to that of the farm. It might cover a hill-side or any irregular ground that is not especially adapted to cultivation, or it might extend along the borders of a stream or lake.

A variety of trees has been recommended, but this does not mean that in suitable places there should not be groves of nut-trees or sugar maples for the production of a valuable crop. One of the delights of a farm should be the gathering of nuts or the making of sugar.

Ordinarily a wood-lot should not be pastured. Pasturing destroys the undergrowth and allows the wind to dry out the ground so that the trees themselves gradually die. An exception might be made to this rule when there is low land along streams, lands subject to frequent overflow and so unsuitable for plowing. Such soil is usually rich and moist and well adapted for pasture. To have scattering tall trees upon this land with a few low-growing hawthorns would not diminish materially its value as a pasture and would make it beautiful. The foliage of hawthorns is eaten to some extent by cattle, but these trees protect themselves sufficiently by their thorns to enable them to increase gradually in size. They not only protect themselves but they frequently protect a bed of adder-tongues, bloodroots, trilliums, hepaticas or anemones underneath their branches.

In situations like that described in the above paragraph, care should be taken to protect the banks of the stream from erosion and at the same time allow the cattle to have a liberal and convenient supply of water. The growth of trees and bushes along concave banks should be protected by fencing. There will usually be some low sloping borders of the stream where cattle may enter it without harm.

In starting a forest or wood-lot, small trees should be chosen. Often it is best to plant year-old seedlings and sometimes acorns or nuts. Trees grow faster than one thinks, and, with a multitude of small trees placed not very far apart, a forest soon develops. The advantages of this method are that all the ground is occupied from the start and all is covered with a mulching of leaves in the autumn which will enrich the land. With such a plantation of small trees, the strongest get the start so that the future forest of large trees will be made up of healthy strong individuals. Such a forest is also beautiful from the beginning. The trees, to a large extent, take care of each other so that the farmer need give them but little attention. Squirrels and other animals would dig for acorns and nuts, so it is often an advantage to plant year-old seedlings.

In addition to planting about the house and other buildings and the wood-lot, the farm has other features that will count in the landscape. Usually, the more or less undulating fields are beautiful. There is beauty in the bare ground, finely pulverized and well prepared to receive the seed for the next crop; in the young green blades, when first seen against the dark earth, and later, when the grown crop waves in the wind, it has something of the charm of a large body of water. The mere mention of wheat, rye, corn, clover, alfalfa and other crops brings to mind something pleasing to look at.

THE FARM ORCHARD AND OTHER FEATURES

Orchards are noted for their beauty, and though they are attractive at all seasons, they are especially handsome when in bloom or when full of fruit. Small-fruits, blackberries, raspberries, currants, goose-berries and strawberries, are often most attractive in appearance.

Also, a farm may have springs surrounded by charming wild growth, creeks, ponds, and lakes. Here and there about a farm there may be individual trees or groups of trees. Every farmer's boy and girl should learn to swim, skate, row, and paddle, either by taking advantage of some body of water connected with their own farm or that of a neighbor, or by going to a township or a county park.

Important though the beauty of the farm may be, there is something of still greater importance, and that is that the farmer and his family shall see and appreciate this beauty. If they can do this, they are of all persons the most fortunate. Other men and women work in their offices, their shops, their factories and their kitchens all their lives until their declining years, when they are likely to seek a home in the country so that they can spend the few remaining years in enjoyment. The farmer can spend not only his declining years but his entire life in enjoying nature. He can always have the trees, bushes and many of the other interesting features that have been named.

When a farmer sees none of the beauty of the country; when he looks on his life as one of drudgery; when he seeks merely to earn dollars and compares his often meager income with that of wealthy men in the city; his declining years are likely to arrive too early in life. He may be old when he has reached the age of forty or fifty. When he sees the beauty of nature; when he realizes the comfort that he enjoys, the satisfaction of breathing pure air, of having freedom beyond that of most men, the pleasure of listening to the songs of birds, looking at the expanse of sky, the beauty of woodlands, of sunrises and sunsets; when he takes a philosophical view of life; when he solves the various farm problems with intelligence and wise foresight; his declining years may be postponed far beyond those of the average man. With the ideal farmer's life, such years may never be reached.

The beauty of the farm, the farm which is the foundation of our prosperity and most of our happiness, leads to that love of country which is true patriotism.

CHAPTER X

LANDSCAPE-GARDENING FOR ARID AND SEMI-ARID REGIONS

SINCE writing the previous chapters, the following communication, which will serve as a text for the present one, has been received from the Editor of the *Rural Science Series:*

"I was standing in the office of one of the educational institutions of a western state looking out at the bare bald hills. A woman in the office who had recently been East, remarked to me that in the part of the country she visited all the hills were spoiled by the forests. She said it was a relief to get back to the West where the hills stood out by themselves, and she could see all the outlines and all the shadows and not have them covered by a mere growth of trees. This raises a very important question for half of the geographical area of our country. What is to be the type of landscape-gardening in the great treeless or semi-arid West where millions of people are going to live? About their homes they will have a little irrigated patch perhaps, but the landscape must be a natural one in all the regions beyond. In many parts of the country they will not even have irrigation about their homes, as they practice dry-farming, which is the process of getting one crop in two years or two crops in three years by such methods of tillage as will save all the rainfall and make use of the moister parts of the year for getting their crops started. From the point of view of the old landscape-gardening these areas seem to be hopeless; yet, numbers of persons must live in these regions and there ought to be some way whereby the artist can develop for them a new type of satisfaction. All our artistic conceptions of landscape-gardening seem to be drawn from humid countries, as, indeed, our common agriculture is so drawn; but more than half of the land surface of the earth receives a rainfall of less than twenty inches and has a set of problems of its own. I often wonder what would be the character of our landscape art if it had been developed first in a semi-arid country."

What can a landscape-gardener do for a treeless region? While he can sometimes improve appearances by grading or by using rocks in an artistic way, his work, to a very large extent, is connected with the growth of vegetation. Ordinarily, he needs trees for shade, for sky-lines and for beauty of foliage, branches, flowers and fruit. He needs shrubs and herbaceous plants for their beauty and to cover the ground, since it is his ideal to have all ground occupied with growing plants excepting that taken by roads, walks, bowlders, and protruding rock. Where plants are lacking, what can be done to make a home comfortable and beautiful?

There is hardly any locality that need be entirely destitute of plants, even though these may be only cacti, yuccas, and sage-brush. The outlines of buildings as silhouetted against the sky are always important, but are of special significance in a treeless region. Usually, buildings in such a region should be broad and low. In arranging buildings for comfort, the prevailing winds and the climate should be studied in the western states just as in the East. In arranging a home in New Mexico or Arizona, which are typical arid states, the points to be considered might be enumerated as follows: —

1. *Views.*

Large areas in New Mexico and Arizona command attractive mountain views. There are also beautifully colored rocks, of all shapes and sizes and, apparently, of endless extent. There are often rolling surfaces supporting at least a slight vegetation, although, to eastern eyes, large areas in these western states seem to be worthless barren wastes. There are persons who delight in the color effects and the immense distances in this region. Houses here, just as in wooded regions, would be placed so that the rooms habitually occupied would command the best views.

2. *Breeze*.

Advantage would be taken of prevailing winds to secure the greatest amount of comfort by placing homes so they will be protected from cold and disagreeable winds, by hills, and also have the advantage of the breezes that add to one's pleasure in summer.

3. *Elevation*.

Even though it may be unnecessary to take any precautions with regard to drainage, high land would naturally be chosen as a site for a house for the sake of air and a commanding view of the surrounding country.

4. *Planting*.

There should undoubtedly be some planting. There must be water to drink and for cooking, to say nothing of bathing, and with water for these purposes enough could probably be obtained for house plants and vines. There should also be a vegetable-garden, and to conserve moisture for this a surrounding growth of bushes would be advantageous. Experiments have shown that even a slight breeze doubles the evaporation from the ground and a strong wind has a marked effect. Bushes, therefore, by checking the wind, help to keep the garden moist so that vegetables, which are important for food, can be grown. The surrounding bushes can be varied in outline, especially along the outer margin, thus making an interesting detail in landscape. It may not be feasible in an arid region to have many trees, but a single specimen, perhaps a pine or a red cedar like those one sees from trains in passing through New Mexico, can usually be so placed with reference to the house as to make a picture for one to look at when approaching the home. Such a tree will also give shade and make the view from a house more interesting.

The problem for a landscape-gardener in any location is to make the most of the available materials. It is wise always to work in harmony with what nature has done in the surrounding territory. In

any locality, whether dry or moist, planting material
should be used which is indigenous to the region or
which grows in some other locality having a similar
soil and climate. In dry sections, as has already
been suggested, use can be made of several species
of shrubs generally known as sage-brush, although
in many cases this is not a correct appellation. In
some dry localities, a cactus garden perhaps in combination with rocks would be appropriate and interesting. There are also numerous herbaceous
plants which come into bloom even in our so-called
desert at certain seasons of the year and which are
exceedingly interesting. These can be used about
one's home as a ground cover and are often attractive even when dry. They do not always make a
suitable carpet to walk on, but paths along the
routes usually traveled may be made with stepping
stones, gravel or any other suitable material that
may be available.

It is unwise to attempt to change Colorado or
Arizona to give them the appearance of Ohio or
Georgia, but much can be done to make the homes
in these and other western states attractive. The
writer has been to western towns when they were
entirely destitute of trees and seemed to him most

forlorn and ugly in appearance. After a lapse of several years, he has again seen these towns containing a growth of shade trees, bushes and flowers. This is an indication of what can be done if there is an inclination to improve appearances. Here as elsewhere the important thing for the landscape-gardener to do is to teach persons to see and appreciate natural beauty. He should also point out the attractive local features, designating how these can be taken advantage of or improved, and stimulate that action on the part of the inhabitants which will give them a feeling of satisfaction and pride in their surroundings. It is certainly a satisfactory state of affairs when each one can think his own locality the best one in the world in which to live. Let the western woman continue to admire the bare plains and mountains which to eastern eyes often seem dreary and forbidding, but point out to her how touches of growth here and there near her house may enhance the mountain view and make her immediate surroundings home-like and attractive.

CHAPTER XI

PUBLIC THOROUGHFARES

A STATEMENT was made at the beginning of this book that its purpose is to help make the country more beautiful. To accomplish this result, nothing will contribute more than the improvement of the condition and appearance of public thoroughfares. It is from these thoroughfares or highways that one sees the beauty of cities, villages, farms, parks, lakes, rivers and woods, as well as that of the highway itself. With the improved physical condition of the roads, the country itself will become more beautiful, because farmers will be more prosperous and so better able to have attractive homes and farms. They will become more appreciative of their surroundings, more reluctant to have disreputable-looking barn-yards or slovenly house surroundings and more anxious to own grounds and farms which the increased number of passers-by will admire.

It is unfortunate that in locating highways better judgment was not exercised. While our system of dividing land into sections one mile square and fractions of sections is admirable for describing land areas, the location of roads on the boundaries of these sections is often a mistake from a practical as well as an æsthetic point of view. Many farmers, on account of section line roads which often go up hill and down, have had to lift all the produce hauled to market many feet unnecessarily and travel many miles farther than would have been the case had the roads been laid out wisely. Some of the mistakes can perhaps be corrected in the building of state roads.[1]

Curved highways, while in most cases shortening the distance to be traveled, and allowing roads on easy grades to be constructed economically, have the additional merit not only of looking better than

[1] A. R. Hirst, State Highway Engineer of Wisconsin, in his Presidential address at the fifth annual meeting of the American Association of State Highway Officials at Louisville, Ky., December, 1919, states, as reported in "Good Roads," that the value of a mile in highway distance saved where there are only one hundred vehicles a day would be $3650.00, which, capitalized at five per cent, would be $73,000.00. If there were two hundred and fifty vehicles, the saving a mile on the same basis would be $182,500.00. It is not at all uncommon for a thoroughfare entering one of our larger cities to accommodate one thousand vehicles or more. For a mile saved on such a thoroughfare the gain would be $730,000.00 or more. With this inducement for making "short cuts," it seems probable that many roads will be changed.

o

straight roads, but also of giving the country as a whole a better appearance. In England, which is usually considered the most beautiful country of its size in the world, nearly all the roads are curved. The beauty of New England is due largely to its curved roads which were made before the United States section laws were adopted. Look at any one of the older roads which was used in advance of the government survey and see how much better it fits the ground and how much better looking it is than the more modern straight highway. As a city develops, some of these original thoroughfares, mere trails at first, usually become its leading arteries.

Even with straight highways laid out with the customary width of sixty-six feet, there is a chance for much variation from a straight line in the road which usually requires only sixteen feet, and it is interesting to see how the lines of travel in unpaved roads are frequently on long graceful curves, perhaps to avoid a valley, the steep part of a hill, or a group of trees or bushes. In many cases it would be wise for the highway commissioners, when they put in concrete, macadam, or brick for a permanent roadway, to follow the easy graceful lines of travel.

Often there would be a gain in economy as well as in beauty by so doing.

The importance of having good drainage, easy grades and solid road-beds is becoming well understood by highway engineers, so no space will be given to these matters here. Where grades change, however, some engineers are inclined to make this change

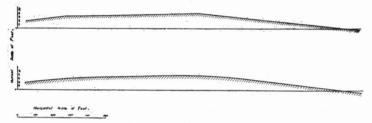

FIG. 42. — PROFILE OF ROAD. The upper profile indicates the character of grades not unusual in cities with long straight sections connected by comparatively short curves. The lower profile is a continuous curve which gives a more satisfactory appearance.

too abruptly, so that the road profile appears angular instead of curved as it should (Fig. 42).

At the road intersections, when for some reason the center lines do not meet, there is an opportunity frequently to use curves to advantage so that there will be a continuous roadway without jogs (Fig. 43). In cities with paved streets and curbs, the radius of curvature of the curb at corners should be long enough so that an automobile can follow the curb closely in turning to the cross street. A radius of at least

twenty feet would be required. This may seem to
be a matter connected with engineering rather than
landscape-gardening, but the landscape-gardener is
concerned with the appearance of the street as a
whole and if it does not fit its purpose, and is not

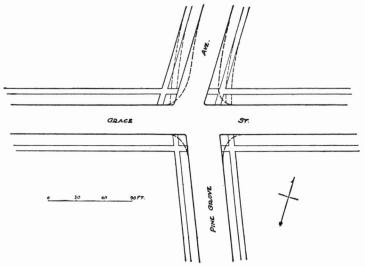

Fig. 43. — The Crossing. This shows in full lines an actual street intersection where roads do not meet, a dangerous arrangement causing conges-
tion. Dotted lines with curves having long radii of curvature show a better
arrangement.

comfortable to use, it will not have a good appearance.

The walk or path along the side of a highway
should have the same freedom that is here advocated
for roadways. Sometimes, in the country, a path

will not be required along the highway, but when it is needed, it should, in most places, be separated from the road by a planted strip of land. The location of the path may be anywhere between the land required for vehicles and the property line. Its grade may be above or below that of the road, provided it is well drained and that it is not crossed by a private drive. For example, if the highway passes along the side of a hill and the foot-path is on the side toward the foot of the hill, its grade may with comfort and safety be lower than that of the road-bed upon which vehicles travel, while the path on the opposite side could be above the road grade, provided always that these paths have profiles that are not too steep. When roads and paths or walks have been constructed with proper lines and grades, planting should be begun. By skilfully using for planting that portion of highways not needed for vehicles or pedestrians, all thoroughfares might be made charming.

Such planting has usually been left to the abutting property owners and, of course, has frequently been omitted altogether. If the appearance of country roads is to become what it should be, the supervision of the planting must be a matter for the highway officials to attend to as well as the construction of the road-bed itself, and these officials should include among their number, or be advised by, a competent landscape-gardener. In some states no attention whatever is given to the planting here advocated, while other states, like New York and Massachusetts, are making intelligent progress. The old idea of having a row of trees on each side of a highway, the trees in the rows being spaced at uniform intervals, is giving way to the more artistic arrangement of groups placed in a natural way. These groups may contain both trees and shrubs. The tree growth may be that of one species or of several, and the same is true of the shrubs and also of the herbaceous material that may contribute to the general effect. With this freedom of arrangement, a wide space between groups may be left where there is a notable view, and again where there is no view the groups may be close together or continuous for a long stretch of highway. By adopting this method, highways might become as attractive as any natural road through the woods. The native species, or those of similar type and character, are to be preferred, both because they match the landscape and because they are hardy and dependable.

THE HILLSIDE ROAD   (Figs. 44 and 45)

A road leads from the city out into the country, its general direction lying from south to southeast. At first it traverses comparatively level land and

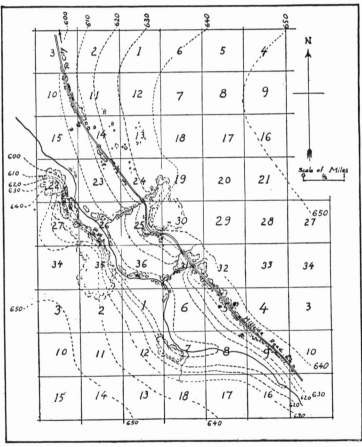

FIG. 44. — A HILLSIDE ROAD.   Often difficult, but full of possibilities.

then enters a valley, bounded on the east or left by a ridge having gradually sloping sides, and on the west by a rather steep bluff. The highway in question follows along the east side of the valley, gradually climbing the broad ridge. The valley is good farming land with pasture and cultivated fields. The time is October. The bluff on the west side of the valley is covered, for the most part, with sugar maples which are brilliantly colored in the morning sun. The broad ridge which the highway is following is old pasture land, some of the fields being thickly sprinkled with hawthorns which the cattle have trimmed into characteristic shapes. Many of these have grown above the browsing line and are covered with red fruits. Little ravines cross the highway and carry surface water underneath through pipes or culverts. At the first point in this mind picture, where the drive begins to follow the ridge, the roadway curves slightly toward the left, and the sloping roadside toward the ridge is covered with Virginia creepers carrying red leaves and dark-bluish berries. Then there is a roadside covering of wild roses with red fruits and dark red stems. On the right, the valley side, is first a group of elms which shade the road and frame the landscape. Continuing toward the south is a spreading group of hawthorns. Beyond the hawthorns there is a long opening through

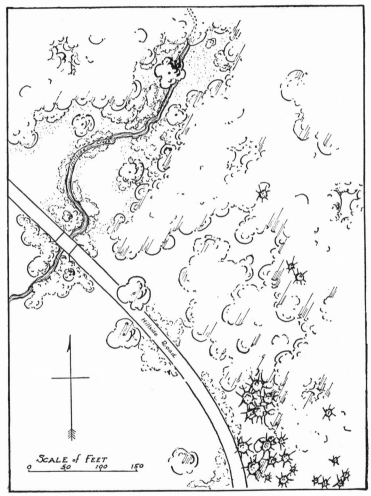

FIG. 45. — THE HILLSIDE ROAD. Sketch of detail of the road.

which the valley is seen, at this point being about a
mile wide. In the valley are green wheat fields in
good condition for the coming winter. There are
other fields containing shocks of corn, farm buildings
nestling among groups of trees and shrubs, and pasture land with scattering herds of cattle. The opening through which these are seen is bounded along
the roadside by a growth of wild roses and elderberries, and is terminated at the south side with an
extended group of sugar maples. After passing the
maples, the road follows a nearly straight course
for some distance, and then turns to the right, but
gradually reverses, passing around a transverse ridge
which is covered with native woods. The growth
seen immediately in front, as one approaches this
turn to the right, is largely composed of hemlocks
and yellow birches. There are also touches here and
there of red-branched dogwoods, and shortly before
reaching the turn there is a ravine which is included
in the woodland and separated from the pasture by
a fence. Looking up this ravine, at the bottom of
which there is a running stream, one can see a large
sycamore with its white trunk. Around the base
of the sycamore and extending up and down the
stream are patches of Indian currants with their

wine-colored berries. One can see also along the sides of the ravine areas of prickly ash, elderberries and wild roses, and, in the distance, a winterberry brilliant with its scarlet fruit. This ravine, extending into the woods at the left, makes a delightful picture. The road continues around the wooded hill in which grow oaks, maples, birches and hemlocks, and as it turns back along the southwesterly slope it passes an attractive farm-house occupying a commanding position with regard to the valley (Fig. 46). This house is framed by great elm trees like the noted elms of New England. The house itself seems to have every appearance of comfort. It not only commands most attractive views, but it receives sunshine and favorable breezes. The elm trees mentioned are along the highway and are flanked by lilacs. Beyond the house, covering the foot of the hill, is an apple orchard which partly screens a group of farm buildings. After passing this scene of domestic comfort and thrift, the road turns to the southeast, skirting the southwest slope of the hill, and crosses another transverse valley. It continues on until the two sides of the valley come together, the character of the country remaining much like that just described. Here and there along the highway are groups of various trees, sometimes a great white oak with an accompaniment of sumachs, sometimes a collection of sugar maples, then a giant black walnut, then a grove of bur oaks flanked with hawthorns, an

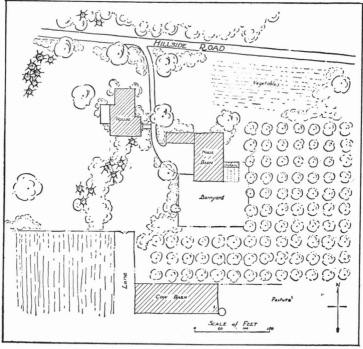

FIG. 46. — THE SCENERY EN ROUTE. Sketch of part of hillside road.

extensive thicket of choke cherries, black haws and tooth-leaved viburnums. Here and there are margins of a bit of woods containing beeches and sugar maples and so on until a distant village is reached.

Growing along the highway, which is often bounded by stone walls, are frequent thickets of hazel bushes interspersed and bordered with goldenrods and asters. Throughout the whole extent of this country road there are beautiful things to look at, trees and shrubs in great variety, often rich in autumn coloring. The road-bed itself gradually ascends to the head of the valley on a grade never exceeding five per cent. It has a smooth hard surface bordered with a strip of land which continues the slope of the road and is covered with grass or other hardy low vegetation, and this, in turn, is bordered perhaps on a steep bank by the growth described. The curves of the road are so easy that an automobile can move safely on high speed and still the beauty of the road itself and the country it traverses is such that it is tempting to one who likes to walk and can take his time to enjoy scenery. While the road is always curved it changes its direction so gradually that approaching vehicles can be seen at a long distance, so that the element of danger is reduced to a minimum.

This imaginary road merely gives a hint of the beauty of a highway which reaches out to a country southeast of a large city, not only of the beauty of the highway itself but also of the country on either side. It reaches the farming district along lines which, though curved, are reasonably direct. The distance along this highway to its destination is much shorter than two straight sides of a right angle, one side of which runs north and south, and the other east and west. Moreover, the cost of the grading, construction and maintenance of the road outlined above would be far less than that of roads constructed through the same country on straight lines.

THE RIVER ROAD   (Fig. 47)

A broad deep river flows southwest from another large city. Within the town the river is traversed by bridges, but in other places it can only be crossed by boats, so that it serves as a barrier for all vehicles and pedestrians. Along the left bank of this river is a ridge of land of which the highest part lies just above high water mark. Back of this ridge the land is relatively low so that during time of extremely high water it is flooded. An indigenous forest growth covers the ridge and its steep banks sloping toward the river and also the low land. Upon the ridge a roadway has been constructed. For a traveler along this roadway the woods furnish constant entertainment. From it, at frequent intervals, and occasion-

ally for long stretches, the interesting opposite bank
of the river is seen as well as the river itself. This
opposite bank is steep and high, reaching in places

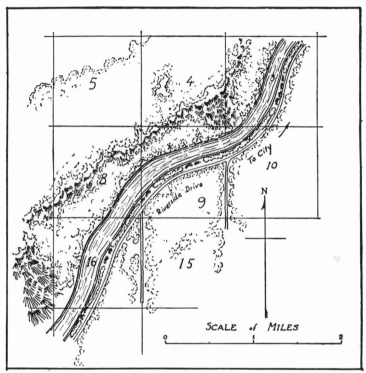

Fig. 47. — A Riverside Drive.   Utilizing neglected opportunities.

an elevation of one hundred feet above the ordinary
river level. It is likewise covered with a forest
growth mostly of oak, but in springtime one could
pick out here and there against the gray mass of stems

the flowers of red-buds, juneberries, wild plums and dogwoods, and near the river a slight yellowish tinge from the blossoms of spice-bush.   A little later there will be light pink areas from the flowers of the wild crab-apple and the leaves of the oaks will appear in various delicate tints.   Sometimes there will be boats upon the river.   The near-at-hand growth along the margins of the river road just mentioned is largely made up of lindens, elms, hackberries, soft maples, sycamores and hawthorns, with here and there a clump of willows.   Underneath the hawthorns, the ground is covered with anemone blossoms in the spring and with little red apples in fall.   Aside from the trees mentioned, there is a growth of various bushes including our red-branched dogwoods, elderberries, spice-bushes, Carolina roses, viburnums and a shrub-like stand of pawpaws.   In places, also, the ground is covered with mandrakes, adder-tongues, bloodroots, hepaticas, trilliums, bluebells, iris and ferns.   This area, mostly covered with original forest extending for several miles along the river, has been converted into a public park.   It is not adapted to ordinary cultivated crops because of the inundations that occur at least once a year and sometimes oftener.

It can be imagined that this river road, with its

varied scenery, will be popular for those who wish to take an after-dinner ride in their automobiles during the long evenings of May, June and July. The words "river road" suggest something interesting. Our native forest growth is becoming every year more and more precious and this forest if preserved for one hundred years or more will be priceless in value.

The birds that frequent the river and the woods will be objects of interest to those who watch for them. The kingfishers will be sure to be on hand and occasionally one will be fortunate enough to see a blue heron, a few ducks or other water fowl. If one goes into the woods and sits quietly in the evening, one may be rewarded with a song of a wood-thrush and at other times in the day one may be fortunate enough to see robins, catbirds, orioles, tanagers, indigo birds, rose-breasted grosbeaks, blue-jays and occasionally cardinal birds. During late spring and early summer, whippoorwills, night hawks and swallows may fill the evening with sound.

From this highway, roads branch toward the south. At first it was thought best to restrict the driving along the river road to pleasure vehicles, but later it was concluded to allow all the farmers who would use this road as the most direct route to

P

the city to have the benefit of the river scenery. In addition to the road, there is a path along the river side for those who wish to walk, and seats have been provided wherever there are favorable outlooks. At two places creeks pass underneath the drive, carrying their supply of water to the river, and the main forest above described has spurs of forest growth extending along the banks of these creeks far out into the country.

There are situations where this imaginary drive might become a reality, giving pleasure forever to the inhabitants of the city who delight in the river drive and also to the farmers who would continue to use it for generations, and toward whose farms the river road makes a direct line of communication from the city. Perhaps, in some instances, a lake might take the place of the river, or the main road might follow the course of a comparatively narrow stream with steep high banks. From such a road branches leading to the farming country might emerge through tributary valleys of smaller size. The aim should be to preserve the natural beauty of the country, while seeking at the same time directness and convenience in lines of travel. By planting in certain places and preserving openings where there

are good views,
one picture after
another will be
presented to the
delighted eyes of
a traveler.

(Fig. 48) THE
PRAIRIE ROAD

The two im-
aginary roads al-
ready described
in outline had
special features
to make them
interesting. One
passed through a
rolling country
with hills and val-
leys and wooded
areas. The other
followed a river,
the banks of
which were also
wooded. The

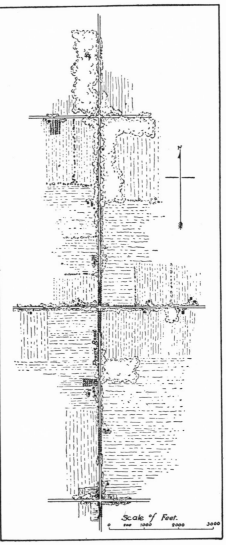

FIG. 48. — THE PRAIRIE ROAD.

third road extends directly north from a prairie town through a country that is almost level, a treeless region with very large farms. What can be done to make such a road interesting? The land stretches in every direction to the sky excepting where the farmers have built homes or planted wood-lots. It may be taken for granted, as one starts out on this road, that it has been built for a long time and the farmers are "old settlers." As this road emerges from town, it leaves a street lined with elm trees which frame in the more open spaces of the country ahead. The roadway itself is a little higher than the adjoining prairie land. It is sixteen feet in width and has a nearly level shoulder on each side. Beyond the shoulder is a depression for surface drainage and beyond the depression near the fence on each side is a path worn by pedestrians. Before reaching the large farms, there are cottages with truck-gardens and a few fruit-trees. Beyond these, in the region of the large farms, planting has added to the beauty and comfort of the thoroughfare. There is a continual growth of low vegetation between the paths on either side and the edge of the roadway. This includes grass, extensive areas of wild roses, aromatic sumach, wild grapes, Virginia creepers, virgin's bower, bittersweet, ironweed, goldenrod, shooting-stars, strawberries, cinquefoils, Jerusalem artichokes, asters and other herbaceous plants. There are also shrubs of higher growth, but these usually appear in a group with certain trees. Soon after leaving town, the road is arched by groups of giant cottonwoods growing on either side, and at the base of these are elderberries. Beyond, near a farm-house, one sees a group of bur oaks. These are not as large as the cottonwoods. It would take another hundred years to bring them to maturity, but they are already beautiful trees, and in time no tree will surpass them in rugged dignity. Some of these trees stand in the highway and others in the front yard of the farmer's house (Fig. 49). At the corner of his yard is a thicket of wild crab-apples, and then along his front line come prairie roses and haw-thorns. Near by, along the highway, is an orchard which helps to carry the sky-line up to the top of the bur oaks, and the growth about the farm buildings is balanced by a wood-lot which has been planted on the opposite side of the road but far enough to the north so that the morning sun will appear early at the farmer's home. This wood-lot, planted by a farmer who had moved from one of the middle

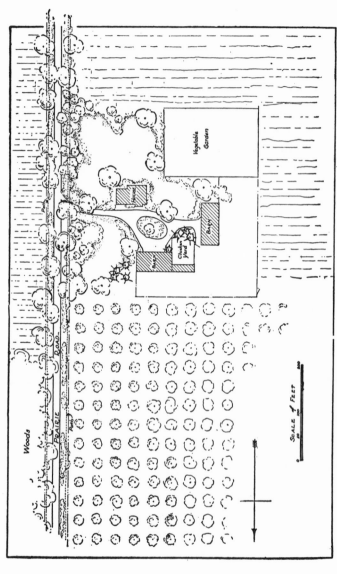

FIG. 49. — THE PRAIRIE ROAD. Detail of road shown in Fig. 48. Dotted lines at sides of roads are paths.

states, was intended to reproduce the character of
the woods with which he had been familiar. Passing this farm-house and wood-lot, one reaches relatively open areas and looks across fields to homes
on various cross roads. Then the road again becomes shaded, this time with sycamores which reach
their untrimmed spreading branches quite across
the roadway as though the trees on one side were
shaking hands with those on the other, and here
again is the same combination that was seen in the
ravine mentioned with the first road, a grouping of
sycamores with extensive stretches of Indian currants.

After passing the sycamores and again looking off
over the surrounding country, the road passes between thickets of hawthorns of perhaps a hundred
different varieties. It would pay one to travel out
from town in the spring to see these hawthorns when
they are in bloom, or again in the fall covered with
fruit and richly colored foliage. Some distance beyond the belts of thorns are thickets of wild plums
leading up to Kentucky coffee trees, and these, in
turn to honey locusts. Protected by one of the wild
plum thickets is a red-bud showing its pink blossoms
above the white flowers of its neighbors. Extending

north from the honey locusts are other trees forming almost an arboretum. These include all the oaks found growing along the rivers or in those wooded areas which exist in nearly all the prairie states. There are many species of oaks, several species of maples, black walnuts, hickories, ash trees, butternuts, lindens, elms, wild cherries, buckeyes and hackberries. With these trees are scattering hawthorns, which appear to have strayed from the main group. Thickets of prickly ash appear here and there and also scattering areas of prairie, meadow and Carolina roses. Many native and some introduced flowers persist in growing along the roadside.

The planting along the highway is sometimes reinforced by wood-lots on either side similar to the one already mentioned. The trees standing between the path and the roadway, that is, occupying a strip lying between six and eighteen feet from the fence, will more than repay by their beauty, shade and protection from wind any harm they may do to the crops in the adjoining fields. These trees as well as the lower growth will furnish places for birds' nests, while the berries and other fruits will serve as dessert for the birds, whose principal meal will be supplied by the insects which the farmer would like to have destroyed. Thus this road continues, extending out from some town, perhaps in central Illinois, and becomes more interesting with each year's added growth.

To be sure, there are long stretches where the crops come to the fences without any interference whatever from the growth in the highway, having a ground-cover along the sides of the roadway consisting of the lower growth that has been mentioned often, not more than two or three feet high. Where the planted wood areas occur, the street planting joins directly on to that of the forest, giving an effect almost equal to natural woods if the planter has been skilful in selecting and arranging the various trees and shrubs.

CITY STREETS

If one enters the city from one of the above de-scribed country roads, one will be fortunate to find a condition so happily described by the late Charles Mulford Robinson as "the country flowing into the city." By this expression he meant the growth of trees, bushes and grass which should extend along the sides of all city or village streets devoted to homes. There are also some factory districts where one finds not only street planting, but park-like grounds for recreation between the factory and the street. The appearance of a city would indeed be greatly improved if there could be less crowding of apartment houses and some more or less public buildings upon the front property lines. Often it would be of great advantage to the appearance of a street if the fence protecting home grounds could be set back so that shrubs could be planted in front of it without encroaching on the sidewalk. This arrangement could often be adopted without any disadvantage to the home grounds. The fence might even be of inexpensive wire entirely hidden by the shrubs on either side, serving as a protection both to the grounds and to the shrubs because it would prevent passing through.

The argument in favor of grouping applies just as well in the city as in the country. If the space for planting is wide enough, varied groups may be introduced. If the space between the curb and the sidewalk is narrow, trees might be planted in rows, but it is not essential that the spacing in this case should be uniform. A wide space may be left to provide a view from a house or from the street across attractive grounds, and where there is no view and no objection to continued shade, the trees may be relatively closer together. Sometimes a space is left in the middle of a street for planting and a roadway constructed on either side. There are some advantages and some disadvantages in this arrangement. The chief advantage is the ample room given for the spread of tree branches and for having effective groupings of shrubs. The disadvantages are the larger expense both for construction and maintenance and the narrowing effect in the appearance of the street. For instance, if the street is narrow with a parkway in the center, the road-bed on either side should be not less than sixteen feet in width, making a total width of pavement for the street of thirty-two feet, while if the road-bed were in the center, twenty-four feet would have as much capacity for traffic as the thirty-two feet in two roads. The appearance of the roadway twenty-four feet wide in the center with ample parkways on either side would be more beautiful and give a more dignified effect than two narrow roadways with the street space divided into two lanes by the planting in the center. With a broad parklike street, having a width of one or two hundred feet, the two roadways would be appropriate, and, with a still wider street, even three roads would be advisable, the center one being for pleasure driving and the side roads for traffic.

In any study of street arrangement for roads, planting and sidewalks, the aim should be to preserve the best effect of space. If possible, the road should be given the appearance of having breadth and freedom. At the corners, the radius of curvature of the edge of the pavement should be at least twenty feet. Sometimes this may cause the sidewalk to meet the pavement on a curved slanting line, but there is no objection to this if the crossing is on a level with the sidewalk as it should be with the surface water removed by catch basins placed along the block instead of at the street intersection.

When a city is on a hill with views out into the country, or when it borders a lake or river, care should be taken not to obstruct street ends (Fig. 50). The city plan should always allow the greatest possible freedom for views outside of the city itself. There will, however, be many advantages in having angular and curved streets within the city boundaries as these will display the architecture or planting to better advantage than long straight streets, and they may fit the topography, reduce cost of construction, and shorten distances. With such planning, there will be effective positions for prominent buildings, such as churches, especially churches with steeples, library buildings, courthouses, hotels, schools and theaters, but if a street commands a beautiful view of a valley, a distant hill, a lake or a river, a school building or any other structure should not on any account be placed where it will cut off this view. Frequently a most exasperating bill-board is put in just such a location.

The discussion of the proper width of streets, the kind of pavement to use, and many other questions connected with construction and main-

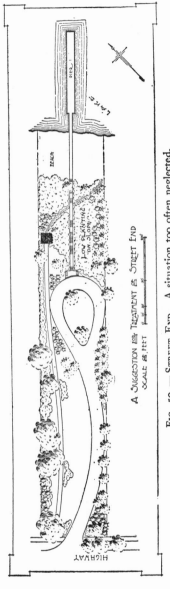

FIG. 50. — STREET END. A situation too often neglected.

tenance is left to city planners and engineers, the special domain of the landscape-gardener or landscape-designer being to protect the appearance of the great out-of-doors. It is his mission to plan the most effective arrangement of trees and other growth, to protect views, hide unsightly objects, preserve sunshine and everything that makes for beauty.

In cities one great obstacle to the development of beautiful streets which does not prevail in the country is smoke. Trees make a city beautiful. Even if the architecture is ugly, as it too often is, large healthy trees would redeem the city. But smoke kills the trees, and although attractive streets and buildings are planned, it will be impossible to have really beautiful cities as long as the atmosphere is polluted with smoke. There is a partial remedy in smoke-preventive devices and in care in feeding coal to furnaces, but probably the most effective prevention of smoke in cities will come with the development of electricity at the coal mines and the carrying of heat, light and power by means of wires instead of on freight trains, trucks, wheelbarrows, and shovels.

BILL-BOARDS

The planting out of ugly features has been recommended, but some are so big that they cannot be obliterated, especially in the limited space available for that purpose. These are the bill-boards which have increased alarmingly in spite of legislation and the efforts of various public-spirited bodies to suppress them. Anything which offends the nose or the ear is at once called a nuisance, but many persons have not yet learned that things which offend the eye are also nuisances. A big glaring sign insists on passers-by spending their money for a certain brand of cigar. If a man stood on the curb calling the same words in a loud voice, he would at once be arrested. The same sentiment ought to exist with regard to bill-boards, that take advantage of streets and parkways which have been built at great expense for pleasant drives and walks. These insolent boards, often two stories in height, face many roadways and public parks, and one cannot approach any large city without having the feeling for beautiful landscape continually offended.

CHAPTER XII

The Grounds of Railway Stations and Rights of Way

WHETHER the grounds about a railway station should be improved by the company or the community may be open to question, but there is no doubt about the wisdom of making these areas attractive. They form the main entrance to a city or village. Strangers are likely to judge a town by its appearance as seen from trains, or from the first impression given by the surroundings of a station. The effect of these surroundings on one who is not a stranger and who sees them continually is important. Their appearance should make him proud of his city.

If the approach to a city from a station is satisfactory, there must be ample room for the accommodation of all vehicles and for a certain amount of embellishment with trees, shrubs, vines, flowers or lawn. There will usually be a combination of all of these in grounds that are ideal.

Some railways have already made a good start
in the right direction. Among these are the Boston and Albany Railway at its stations near Boston, the Pennsylvania Lines at many of their suburban stations, the Michigan Central at a few of
its stations, and some others. Sometimes a railway has made an attempt to have beautiful station
grounds without securing a satisfactory result.
Perhaps a circular bed of flowers has been planted
in the middle of a lawn near the platform, while
back of this there are ugly sheds, buildings or obtrusive bill-boards. The effect from the station
should take into account all the surroundings, including the buildings, the streets, and the planting.
If the buildings are ugly, they might be improved
by paint, or by planting trees so as at least partially to hide them, or they might be torn down
and the ground they occupied included with the
station property so as to make the whole effect
attractive and dignified. A careful study of the
grounds, with plans made by some skilful designer,
should not only lead to a satisfactory welcome,
but to real economy in maintenance and to increased valuation in adjoining property.

In designing station grounds, the first essential

Q

is to plan for convenience, so that persons coming to the station, whether in vehicles or on foot, will reach it in an easy natural way. There should be ample room to unload passengers along the platform, or to receive them as they come from trains. If there is any angle about the station building not used, it can be occupied with vines, bushes, or perhaps a tree. If a city street adjoins the grounds of the station, perhaps the farther side can be planted rather thickly, and the near side kept relatively open, the resulting space being broadened by the combination and giving a dignified effect. If the station grounds adjoin private property, any unsightly buildings or fences thereon should be planted out (Fig. 51). A thick plantation of shrubs such as lilacs, syringa bushes, viburnums or thickly branched trees, like hawthorns, would be suitable for this purpose, and such growth would make a desirable background for flowers. Often, in planting flowers, it would be wise to select perennials, since the cost of their maintenance would be small and also they would be effective during a greater part of the year. Goldenrods, for example, are often attractive even when dead and brown. Their graceful shapes, especially when partly cov-

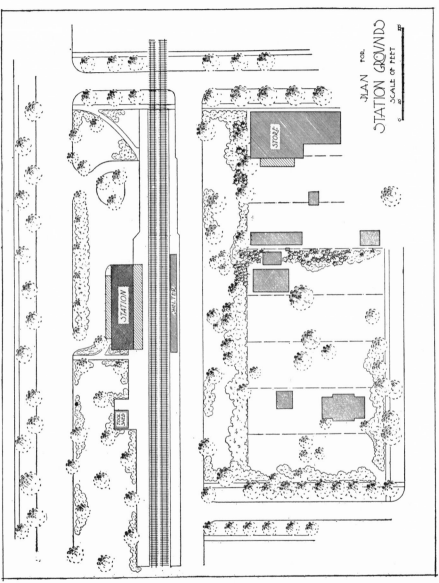

FIG. 51. — THE RAILROAD LANDSCAPE.   Plan for small suburban station grounds.

ered with snow, would be tempting to any pho-
tographer. Many other perennial plants are attractive even when their stems are dead, and the
seeds which they produce often furnish food for
birds in the winter. Evergreens would be suitable
for planting if the atmosphere were free from smoke.
Such would be the case about the stations along
electric lines if the towns where these stations are
located produced no smoke. Eventually, when
all lines become electrified, one may hope for ideal
conditions.

Sometimes stations adjoin small parks or are
near river banks or opposite lakes. Such locations are especially fortunate, and advantage should
be taken of the opportunity to secure interesting
views of natural scenery as seen from the station or
from cars.

Railway employees, ticket agents, freight agents,
train hands and others should be taught to see such
beauty as exists about the railway stations and along
the rights of way. This will add pleasure to their
lives and lead to greater contentment. An employee should regard the property of his company as partly his own. Its appearance is certainly
a matter of concern to him, and it is fortunate if

he can obtain pleasure from looking at it during
his daily work and have a feeling of pride when he
mentions it to one of his friends.

The railway right of way, usually one hundred
feet or more in width, offers a great opportunity
for making the country beautiful. The entire right
of way should always be utilized. The central
part of it will be needed for road-beds, bridges,
and tracks. Certain areas along the sides of the
tracks will sometimes be used by employees for
gardens. Such use should be encouraged, but a
vast area of unoccupied land still remains which
should grow something attractive to look at. This
does not mean that railway companies should plant
all this area. Nature will generally take care of the
planting, but railway companies should keep their
men with scythes away from it. A few examples
will call to mind successful efforts on nature's part.
There are places in northern Wisconsin where
the ground along the side of the railways is covered
in spring with the white flowers of bunchberry, and,
in autumn, with the beautiful red berries of this
charming little dogwood. Similar areas are covered
with the pink and white blossoms of shooting-star.
Along various lines in Michigan and other north-

ern states, in marshy places far below the tracks, the ground will be covered very early in the season with the yellow flowers of marsh marigold, and later with the leaves and flowers of wild iris. Perhaps a few of our native lilies will show their heads in midsummer. Along certain lines near the sand dunes of Indiana, the land is sometimes covered with the white, blue, and purple flowers of lupine. Wild roses, ironweed, wild asters, goldenrod, black-eyed Susans, sunflowers, dewberries, and hundreds of other attractive plants will decorate the land seen from the window of a railway coach if they are only given an opportunity. The railway right of way might indeed become a great botanic garden where plants take care of themselves and select the situations best adapted to their growth. Often they serve this purpose at the present time, but they might do so to a greater extent if the matter were given a little thoughtful consideration.

To be sure, one must consider the fact that sparks will fly from locomotives and will sometimes start fires. Much, however, can be done or left undone to encourage the wild garden or botanic garden that has been mentioned without increasing the fire risk. The wild gardens should exist along all rights of way where the space is not needed for side-tracks or other purposes. When all railway trains run by electric power, the danger from fire will be negligible and then the list of allowable plants will include many shrubs and small trees. Such sometimes grow along the lines of electric roads at the present time and produce an effect that is charming and gives pleasure to travelers.

When nature, with man's assistance, or, in certain cases, with his non-interference, can decorate the banks of all streams, the borders of all highways, and all vacant land included in railway rights of way, the country will become so beautiful that people from other lands will wish to see it and its own citizens will derive pleasure each day from looking at it and from that feeling of contentment that comes with the ownership of beautiful objects and with seeing things well done.

To bring about some of the results suggested, it is necessary that some of the railway officials should be imbued with a desire to have these results and with that vision which is the first requisite of any worthy undertaking.

CHAPTER XIII

Parks, Forest Preserves, City Squares

As in attempting any project, the one who essays to design a park should first have the main purpose it is to serve clearly in mind. There are many opinions as to what this purpose is. The man who is fond of boating thinks the park is for the purpose of giving him an opportunity to take his favorite exercise. He wishes the golf course excavated to enlarge the yacht harbor. The golfer, on the other hand, desires the harbor filled up to enlarge his golf course. The equestrian thinks the park is a place for bridle paths, the horseman for a race course, the gardener for flowers, the public-spirited man, at others' expense, a place for a statue of his friend or a public building in which he is interested. The advertiser thinks the parks and the boulevards are the most appropriate sites for his bill-boards. A gardener argued that his "Gates Ajar," sundial, elephant, and roll of carpet made out of alternantheras, echeverias, and other bedding plants were the most interesting and valuable features of a park because the most persons came to see them. Frederick Law Olmsted, the greatest authority on parks whom the United States has produced, made the very apt reply, "more people go to a circus than to an art gallery." The number of persons who think that a park should contribute to their special hobbies is most exasperating.

Dwellers in cities grow tired and large numbers to recuperate seek the country, the woods, the ocean, lakes, rivers, mountains, in short, nature. There are many, however, who cannot afford either the time or the money to go to the country and so the country should be brought to them. This means that the parks, which every large city should have, must partake as far as possible of the character of the country. Sometimes one wishes to get away from people and have only trees, bushes, and birds for companions. A park should give this opportunity for quietness and rest. Again, many persons will have a desire to leave brick walls, paved streets, and the noises of a city and enjoy natural scenery just as they might wish to look at pictures in an art gallery. A park should furnish such scenery and be in restful contrast to busy streets.

A few features that exist or have existed near cities might here be noted. In the outskirts of one city is a stream which has worn its way deep into a bed of limestone rock. At the upper edge of the often overhanging rock, thirty or forty feet above the bed of the stream, the ground slopes back and is covered with trees. This slope is very steep and could not be used for crops or buildings. The trees and vines spreading out over the irregular rocky cliff made with the stream below a beautiful picture. Many admired this picture and wished that the stream, the rocks and the trees might belong to the city and be included in a park so that they could be preserved for all time, but the owner of the land thought the trees had value as wood and cut them down.

A city is located in a valley a mile or two in width, this valley being bounded by high bluffs or hills. These hills were originally wooded. A portion of one of the hills was purchased by a public-spirited citizen and given to the city for a park. In other parts the bluffs have been scarred by rectangular

streets, necessitating enormous cuts, the destruction of all the trees and, for a long series of years, a
barren, forlorn appearance.

The destruction of streams which were once
attractive and which might have been made the
most interesting features of parkways and parks
has already been referred to.

Innumerable other instances might be given of
the needless destruction of natural scenery, which
is always to be regretted, and especially so when this
scenery is within the boundaries of or near a large
city.

From the facts mentioned above and from others
that will come to the mind of any intelligent,
thoughtful person, it will probably be conceded
that the main purpose of a park is to preserve, restore, develop, and make accessible natural scenery. In some ways a park may be an improvement
on nature, since, by skilful treatment, it may be
made more picturesque or more artistic than if
nature had been left untouched. A park is not
primarily a place for play, but rather to feed one's
soul. Its chief purpose may be illustrated by the
following incident. A man who had lived to middle
age in an inland town visited a city with parks

located on the shores of a large body of water. He had never seen water extending beyond the range of vision. On going out to one of the parks and walking along the shore, he was filled with awe as he sat for a long time watching the big waves roll in. He was charmed by what he saw and greatly impressed by the power of the waves and the boundless expanse. Such an experience is not to be measured by dollars. It is priceless. A somewhat similar feeling may be experienced by one who visits a stretch of woods of apparently unlimited extent, or by one who looks over a park scene containing a valley in the foreground, with hills or mountains miles away far beyond the park boundaries.

Remembering that a park is a place to show natural scenery, it will be granted that this scenery will be observed from different points of view. One will wish to stop at certain places where the views are especially good, and there seats should be provided. In going about, one will either walk upon paths or lawns, or ride in wheeled vehicles upon drives, or on horseback upon bridle paths, or in boats upon lakes or streams. Where one goes in boats in summer one may skate in winter, and also coast if there are hills. The walks and drives are primarily for convenience, for use. The lawns and water are primarily for beauty, but, incidentally, the water may be used for boating or skating, or, if conditions are favorable, for swimming, and the lawns for tennis, croquet, and certain other games or sports.

It will thus be realized that while parks exist, as has been stated, primarily for beauty, they give at the same time opportunities for delightful exercise as well as rest and enjoyment. The trees furnish shade, the flowers color and perfume, the space freedom and grateful breezes. The lawns, the trees, and shrubs also give interesting and pleasing compositions in color and outline.

PLANNING A PARK

With parks fulfilling the purpose which has just been named, it will be seen that they can be of almost any size or shape. Their location will be influenced, first, by existing natural objects. Forests, hills, especially if wooded, river banks, the shores of lakes, ravines, springs, streams, and rocky ledges are all desirable features, and a city where such features exist is indeed fortunate if it can secure the land they occupy for public use as a park.

Accessibility should also be taken into account in selecting locations for parks, but the character of the land is of greater importance, as one can easily travel a long or short distance.

Assuming that a city, with the assistance of a landscape-gardener, has secured one or more tracts of land and placed this under the control of a park commission, the next step would be the making of suitable plans for park development. A park might be planned directly on the ground it occupies by a skilful landscape-gardener, but, usually, it is advisable to have a topographical survey and plat made so that one, by looking at this, can obtain a comprehensive idea of the extent and lie of the land, the area covered by forest and by any existing water, marsh, cultivated ground or rock. Even with such a plat, it is advisable to study the land itself, noting all the features of special interest, the views outside of the park as well as those within its limits, and the favorable locations for such walks and drives as may be needed. The directions given with regard to walks and drives in home grounds will usually be applicable in a public park. The designer should always remember that drives and walks are for use, that they should go where persons wish to travel, and there should be as few of them as possible while meeting these requirements. Advantage will, of course, be taken of all existing growth, and in selecting plants for such additional growth as may be required, those varieties which harmonize with existing vegetation and are suitable for the soil will be chosen. The designing of the park will consist mostly in picturing to one's mind attractive compositions that will fit the situation and take advantage of existing features.

Since parks may have a wide range of sizes, shapes, and locations, there will be many kinds of problems involved and at least as many solutions. In general, a park should partake of the character of the country in which it is located. The designer should, therefore, study not only the site of the park itself, but also any native woods that may be in its vicinity, as well as the different soils and the hills, valleys, rocks, and other topographical features of the surrounding region. Such a survey will often disclose valuable planting material that may be available for the park, and also give useful hints as to what the character of the planting should be. Frequently a study of existing woods will call attention to pleasing combinations of plants, satisfactory grades, beautiful sky-lines, interesting boundaries for spaces, all of which will give useful hints in designing the park.

If the tract selected for a park is covered or partly so with native forest, it is fortunate. In this case, the removal of some growth will doubtless be needed. Some trees and bushes must be removed to open up views, others because they are partially or wholly dead, others since they interfere with the proper development of better growth, and still others just to make a beautiful picture. This work cannot be done or planned in an office. It requires the skill of a landscape-gardener on the ground, and the selection of plants to be taken out should never be left to the wood choppers. A landscape-gardener should visit the land before it is selected for a park if possible, but if he cannot do that he should at least see it before any work is done on it. The need of this may be illustrated by an incident. A landscape-gardener was engaged to design a park and on going out to see the land with the park commissioners, he was told that he had come just in time. "You can have everything your own way," they said to him, "we haven't done a thing," then, after a pause, "ex-

cepting to cut out the underbrush." The "underbrush" was found to have been most beautiful
masses of prairie roses, elderberries, and pawpaws. It is a fact that what is often called "underbrush" is sometimes more valuable than the tree
growth from a designer's point of view. He should
pass on the relative value of different natural or
existing features of the land purchased. It is
wise to make use of existing plants or other material
of value on the land acquired instead of destroying
these and replacing them with something no better
or perhaps not as good.

Sometimes the problems connected with a park
may relate only to the thinning out and planting,
as in those cases in which the park is small or occupies a long narrow hillside, perhaps between a
highway and a river, or a steep rocky bluff on the
opposite shore almost inaccessible, and seen only
by those who look across the river or from boats.
In such parks, if any artificial features are called
for, they will include only paths, seats, and perhaps a shelter or lookout. No grass will be needed,
but the ground cover will be bushes, vines, herbaceous plants and leaves. In places rocky ledges
and boulders may be exposed.

R

With parks of somewhat larger area and greater width but still of moderate size, lawns and walks will be introduced, but if there is a street along at least one side of the park, probably no drive into or through it will be required.

With still larger areas, drives will be introduced at first relatively near the boundary so as to leave large, uninterrupted, open spaces centrally located. These drives are for the purpose of helping those who ride to see the scenery of the park. In places, such drives will pass through wooded areas, then emerge into the open, perhaps on an elevation of land commanding a view of an extensive lawn or lake within the park, or a range of hills or other object of interest far beyond its boundary. Thus a park drive will be given variety, making it interesting in itself as well as placing it where it will command views of the scenery for which the park exists.

GROUNDS FOR GAMES OR RECREATION

As parks increase still further in size, there can be no doubt as to the propriety of allowing such sports as tennis, croquet, and the less strenuous games of ball to be played on the more extensive lawns, but football, excepting as played by small boys as a mere pastime, belongs in an athletic field or playground, and there may be some question as to baseball.

Park commissioners are justified in hesitating to allow golf to be played in a park. They should first consider the paramount object in having a park, which is the development and preservation of scenery that is nature-like in appearance for the recreation of all and especially those persons who cannot go to the country. A park exists for everybody without regard to the amount of taxes paid. It resembles the schools in that respect. In the schools a child of the poorest family has just as many privileges as one of wealthy parents and it is right that it should be so. The stability of the country and the security in which we live depend on the training and education of all the children to insure their becoming good citizens. The parks also help in the same direction. They are educational and ought to be more instructive than they usually are by having intelligent employees who could point out to visitors matters that are of educational value. It would be ideal to have every employee in the park able to give a questioner the name of any tree, shrub or flower. Since a park is provided for all who wish to visit it, the commissioners should not allow golf, when, by doing so, they deprive many persons of the privilege of using land which is needed for picnics, for rest, or for indulgence in those quiet games which require little room and which are accompanied by no element of danger such as being hit by a golf ball. On the other hand, when a park is very large in extent, the commissioners would be justified in allowing golf, since by so doing there would be no interference with the usual recreation which the park affords. A great stretch of lawn, perhaps half a mile or more in extent, an expanse that is really needed for the park scenery, may be even more interesting if dotted with players.

The introduction of certain sports into parks has sometimes been justified by the statement that they would bring more persons to the park. Some have even attempted to introduce race-tracks, which are entirely out of harmony with the spirit that should prevail in a park. For those who really need a park, it is an advantage not to have it crowded. Horse racing, polo playing, football, circuses, gatherings to listen to public speaking, and in general all features which tend to collect a crowd having little or no interest in the park scenery should be rigidly excluded.

In all parks of comparatively large size and in those boulevards or parkways which have sufficient breadth, bridle paths may be introduced with propriety. Horseback riding is a pleasant and healthful exercise and is a mode of travel which gives the riders an advantageous outlook. They usually go at a leisurely pace which gives them time to see the combinations of open space and wooded areas to advantage, and they may easily stop and inspect any view or object which interests them. Moreover, equestrians with their horses are usually interesting to pedestrians and others who are taking their recreation in different ways. Bridle-paths may with advantage be varied in width. Where there is ample space the width may allow several to ride abreast, and again where the room is more limited, the width can be narrowed so that only one line in single file can meet a similar line going in the opposite direction. A path may even be divided into two or more parts for the sake of saving trees and bushes and giving an interesting variety to the bridle-path itself.

The buildings introduced into a park should be

strictly limited to those which minister to the comfort of visitors. Shelters, an office building, comfort stations, bath-houses, boat-houses, restaurants, and band-stands are legitimate. Sometimes two or three of these buildings can, with advantage, be united in one. Such structures, however, should be subordinated to the general landscape effects. They should not be more conspicuous than a group of trees. They should be conveniently located to serve their different purposes, usually near a walk or drive, but never out in the open.

When a park is favorably situated, that is, when it has an abundant supply of water, it is well to give opportunity for swimming. Swimming is one of the delights of the country wherever there is a lake, creek or river, and city boys and girls should be given the same opportunities that their country cousins enjoy. Boating and canoeing should also be provided for when the conditions are at all favorable. These are not only healthful exercises, but they give one an opportunity to see overhanging trees and the delightful effects that should exist along the banks of lakes and streams.

OTHER PURPOSES OF A PARK

There are so many pleasurable ways of exercising and playing in a park that one sometimes forgets the fundamental reason for acquiring land and going to the expense of planting, making roads, walks, and introducing the other features which have been mentioned. There are, however, many incidental purposes that may be served by a park in addition to those named and to the main purpose of preserving nature. A park may serve as an arboretum with collections of many kinds of trees and shrubs. It might also have a botanic garden or a planting of some special kind, such as a Japanese, medicinal, iris, or rose garden. Such gardens, however, should be placed by themselves and not interfere with the general scenery of the park.

A zoölogical garden may sometimes be introduced, but in this case it would be well to have the zoölogical part the main feature, the garden being subordinated to the zoo instead of the zoo to the garden. A zoological garden or park should, if possible, be large enough to give buffalo, deer, and other grazing animals a chance to get at least a portion of their food in the natural way. Frequently the room is so limited that what should be the deer or buffalo pasture becomes merely a piece of bare, muddy or dusty ground.

There are organizations of various kinds, such as gun clubs, natural history societies and others, that will seek to appropriate parts of parks to their own uses. A museum may with advantage be near a park, but should not be intruded within the park itself. The noise of a gun club seems quite out of harmony with the legitimate purposes of a park, and it is only on rare occasions that a suitable site for the operations of such a club can be found. If there should be a point of land extending out from a park into a large body of water to a place far removed from dwellings and from most of the park visitors and protected also by a hill or embankment which would deaden the sound, an exception might be made to the general rule of exclusion.

THE PARK COMMISSION

The park commission should be small, preferably made up of not over five members. At least one large city in the United States has a park commission of only three members. A commission should be practically continuous by having only one member selected each year to serve for a definite term of as many years as there are members of the commission. A man chosen for a commissioner should have some leisure in order that he may find time to learn the duties of his office and the requirements of a park. He should have no interest connected with the park excepting that of rendering the best service to the public. An instance of what should not happen may be given here. Along the boundary of a park in a western city was a beautiful group of evergreens. Across the highway, opposite the evergreens, a man had his home. He wished to have the trees cut down so that he could look into the park. The park board was opposed to cutting the evergreen boundary. The man who lived opposite sought and eventually obtained a position as member of the board, with the avowed object of cutting down the evergreens. He succeeded in accomplishing his purpose, but to his own regret, for he found afterwards he had destroyed the privacy of his own home. An intelligent unbiased commissioner would have known that a park should be separated as far as possible from the built-up portion of the city.

It is a trite saying that a park should be divorced

from politics, but unfortunately there are many cases where this lesson has not been learned. A good commissioner serves the public from a sense of patriotism and not on account of patronage or perquisites connected with the office. He should be a lover of nature, a man of taste, and a sympathizer with all good things connected with the park.

FOREST PRESERVES

In many respects forest preserves near cities are like parks. They are similar in purpose and character. Both have trees, shrubs, and flowers. Both include large areas. The area in forest reserves should be much larger than that included in the city's park system. A forest reserve should be procured within a reasonable distance of every city and should be preserved as natural forest. One's feeling with regard to such a native forest should be similar to that which one might have for the preservation of Indian mounds or any other existing feature connected with Indian life, or to preserve undisturbed any historical spot. The forests with their trees, their undergrowth and wild flowers, are the oldest things in existence next to the earth itself. What a possession that city will have, say, in five hundred or a thousand years, which can point to a tract covered with trees and other native growth and say, "that is a tract of original forest; it has been preserved as the Indians left it."

A forest makes an appeal because it is beautiful and has something of mystery about it. It is nature's own creation, but if it is to be preserved it must be carefully guarded. The water level must not be lowered. The underbrush must not be cut out. The covering of decaying leaves must not be disturbed. The wild flowers must not be picked. Provisions should indeed be made for visiting a forest, but when one enters he should have a feeling like that of the religious man who visits a cathedral. He should go with reverence and take away with him not wild flowers and broken branches of trees and shrubs, but a remembrance of the beauty and fragrance of the forest, an appreciation of the birds which he has seen, a recollection of the fresh pure air, the sunshine, or perhaps a storm, a feeling that he has had communion with nature and has been refreshed and rejuvenated.

If, in acquiring the forest land, it is necessary to take certain cleared or cultivated areas, these might be treated in a way to give the greatest satisfaction and pleasure. Open areas can be allowed to become forest, or they may be used for gardens, arboretums, playgrounds or kept as farms to provide food for such animals as are used in the preserve. The forest might be treated in such a way as to grow valuable timber. It is reported that some cities in Europe have usually derived an income from their forests sufficient to pay the cities' expenses so that it has been unnecessary to levy taxes.

The question of roads through a forest would be determined by local considerations. Roads in certain places might serve as a protection against fire. They would also be useful in hauling out logs and brush from trees that have been cut, but a multiplicity of roads for the general public is hardly to be desired. The main thoroughfares might preferably be located outside of the forest itself, with the exception of certain cross roads when a forest is quite long in a direction at right angles to the main lines of travel. Usually seedlings of trees that belong in the vicinity should be planted in a forest; for example, if white pines had once existed in a forest but had been removed for the lumber they would produce, it would be wise to introduce this tree again, and the same would be true of any species which had formerly grown in this or in neighboring forests. The paths should be merely wood paths, usually covered with last year's leaves. They should lead to such shelter houses as may be necessary and to the best places for observation.

CITY SQUARES AND TRIANGLES

A city is fortunate if, in laying out the streets, little areas of land are left here and there where trees can be planted. Often, if there is a triangle, it will be unnecessary to cross it with a walk. In such cases, the center might be planted with trees, and from all points of view on streets approaching the triangle, these trees would help to make a picture. City squares often tempt pedestrians to make diagonal paths and it is usually wise to provide walks substantially along lines of travel. A big circular fountain or other obstruction in the middle of one of these walks is usually an unfortunate arrangement. Fountains, statues, or other ornamental features should be placed at one side of the direct lines of walks. A square might be graded and planted so that a slightly curved walk would seem natural and be one that would give a good appearance. These small vacant areas, scattered through a city, and relieving the monotony of its street, and buildings, are seen in winter fully as much as in summer. They should, therefore, be planted to look well at all times of the year. Large areas in bedding plants or annuals which leave merely patches of bare ground from October until May are manifestly unsatisfactory as well as expensive. If there were no smoke, evergreens could be chosen and would be especially effective in winter. When conditions are unfavorable to evergreens, small trees and deciduous shrubs would be suitable. When there is room, no deciduous growth is more attractive throughout the year than that of hawthorns, and a group of these trees may be admirable. They may be used advantageously in combination with a tree of large size, like an elm or an oak, and also in combination with lower growth like that of roses, Indian currants, and aromatic sumach. Perennial herbaceous plants producing attractive foliage or flowers would also be suitable and might have the woody growth for a background. Early spring flowers, crocuses, snowdrops, scillas, bloodroots, hepaticas, daffodils,

and many others would make these areas, which
might have any shape, attractive during March,
April, and May. The leaves and flowers of the
trees and shrubs that might be selected would carry
the attention throughout the summer season, and
the fruits and autumn foliage would be features of
special interest during the fall months. From
November until March, the woody branches would
be interesting from their manner of growth and also
from their brown, gray, green, red, or other distinctive coloring. Some hawthorns, as well as some
viburnums, barberries, and roses, carry fruits well
through the winter.

It might be possible even with an atmosphere
more or less polluted to have some bedding plants,
provided they could be so placed as to look well
with the hardy growth and could have their places
taken by evergreens as soon as frost arrives. Individuals do not hesitate to spend large sums for
evergreen window-boxes and other evergreen decoration for winter, and cities would be justified in
going to some expense for the evergreens even if
they were to last but a comparatively brief period,
the pleasure received from such planting being fully
equal to that from a bed of geraniums or begonias.

The questions to be answered by the landscape-gardener when designing these so-called city squares are the same that must be met in regard to most of his other work, namely, what will serve the convenience of the persons for whom the design is made? What will give the most pleasure for a given amount of expenditure? What will make for beauty in connection with the objects surrounding a "square"?

COUNTRY PARKS

City parks and squares have until recently received more consideration from the public than has been given to country parks. It has been argued that those living in the country have nature close at hand, with plenty of sunshine and fresh air, and so do not need parks. Notwithstanding this argument, there are many places even in the country which should be preserved for the use of the public. Some of these have already been mentioned, namely, the borders of streams and lakes and steep hillsides.

Any notable, natural feature should be preserved. Often an individual farmer may have on his land a spring, a wood-lot, a ravine, a great bowlder, an Indian mound, or other object in which he delights and which he takes pleasure in showing to his friends. While he lives this is sufficient, but when he dies the land may be owned by someone who cares nothing for the features named and they may be destroyed. If interesting objects or localities belong to the public, the chances for their preservation for future generations will be better.

TOWNSHIP PARKS

There might be formed in every township a society for the preservation of the native landscape. Such a society, by proper legislation, might be given a legal status so that it could hold the title to such land as might be acquired by donation or otherwise. With such an organization, it ought to be possible to have interesting township parks, that is, wooded areas, the valleys of streams, lake margins, ravines, or hills, level areas for games, swimming pools or other interesting features found within the township boundaries. Such parks would furnish delightful places for picnics or other outings, spots which formerly existed in abundance on private farms, but which are being destroyed by the growing intensity of farming and the increase in population. The outings which one takes are the things that count in life. They make life worth

s

while, and suitable provision should be made for them, not one hundred miles or five hundred miles away, but near at hand. Often there are delightful natural areas near at hand which persons do not see.

A society for the preservation of native landscape, perhaps with the assistance of a landscape-gardener or some amateur nature lover, should point out and secure such places as have been named. Ordinarily, a man works steadily throughout the year with the exception of a short period when he has his "vacation," and then he spends the money he has saved up and a part of his "vacation" in traveling to some distant "resort." Perhaps it would be possible to have just as attractive "resorts" near at hand and have more frequent vacations with all of the time spent in really living. The frequent vacations might be short, Saturday afternoons and Sundays, but they would be restful and enjoyable.

COUNTY PARKS

There should be a friendly adjustment between townships and counties in the matter of parks. Some may think that township parks will answer all purposes, but occasionally there may be some natural feature, a wooded ridge, a river, a lake or a forest, extending through two or more townships which might with propriety be acquired or set aside by county commissioners or by a board of supervisors as a county reserve. Such parks should be planned primarily for the purpose of preserving attractive natural features but incidentally certain parts might be used for camping. Tourists who live in automobiles might find these parks convenient places for stopping over night. As in the case of township parks, they would furnish places for picnics, to which excursions might be made by parties from the city. Certain large areas might be carried on as county forests with the object of conserving the lumber supply and making a profit for the county.

The establishment of county parks would tend to disseminate among all the inhabitants the idea of having public parks. This object would be discussed at the meetings of county officials and the ideas presented would in this manner reach all of the township officers. The establishment of township and county parks would not be justified unless they were used and approved generally. A discussion of such parks at public meetings would tend to bring about a general knowledge and approval of this proposed feature of public life, which would add to the joy of living.

STATE PARKS

The desirability of having state parks may be illustrated by considering a state having a certain amount of frontage on a large body of water like the ocean. The interior counties would have no such frontage, but the dwellers in these counties would desire to visit the ocean. A state park would give them the privilege of doing so without trespassing on private property or paying exorbitant prices for the privilege of looking at the sea. Instead of the ocean, states might have other natural features that should be preserved for the benefit of all its people. Each state, for example, should have large areas of forest to be used for the combined objects of recreation and the production of lumber.

The province of the landscape-gardener in regard to township, county, and state parks would be to advise in regard to the location, the areas to be included, and the treatment required. He should be able to see their natural beauty and point this out to those who are less observant. He should suggest changes that will make them more picturesque, more useful in the lines named. His suggestions would include advice with regard to the location of roads and walks, regarding cutting certain trees or areas of trees, and planting for the purpose of making parks more beautiful or increasing the variety of growth. He would also advise with regard to the treatment of water, rocks, or any other natural features of interest, and suggest ways in which parks might be used without injury and to the greatest pleasure of all.

NATIONAL PARKS

Most interesting books have been written about these parks and the government has issued instructive bulletins regarding them. The size of this book does not permit of their discussion in any detail and they are mentioned here only for the purpose of expressing approval of them and also with the hope that such parks may be established in the older portion of the United States as well as in the Rocky Mountains and coast regions. The idea of having such parks was a grand one and the country is most fortunate in possessing so many large areas set aside for public recreation and for places of refuge for life of all kinds. Future national parks should include areas of sand dunes with frontage on the Great Lakes, areas of forest distributed through parts of the country east of the Rocky Mountains all the way to the Atlantic Ocean, areas in the northern and in the southern states. Let us preserve samples of all the wooded areas and all the natural attractions which our children, grandchildren, and all the generations yet to come will be glad to see. Do not let any portion of the country through lack of forests degenerate to the conditions of certain parts of Spain and other countries that have been denuded of woods.

CHAPTER XIV

Golf Grounds

THE work of the landscape-gardener might almost be described by the definition of golf, "something to make walking interesting." On this account the actual game of golf need not be especially interesting to the landscape-gardener, because he really does not require the exercise to keep him well, but the golf grounds with their broad expanse of open green-covered fields and their unusual opportunities for producing beautiful landscape effects do make such an appeal. Usually the lines of the fair greens leave certain unused areas, often triangular pieces of ground of perhaps half an acre or more in extent. Such triangles offer opportunities for effective planting.

Occasionally one or more large-growing trees may be planted near the tees and give grateful shade to those who are waiting for a chance to play. Sometimes, when the grounds are large, they may include a stream or a lake, with opportunities here and there along their banks in stretches between the fair greens for some shrubs or vines. The vicinity of the club-house requires much study and planning in order to produce the best landscape effect. The club-house is in some respects like a home, and the approach drive should be developed along the same lines that would be adopted by an individual. Usually the verandas of a club-house will be larger, however, than those of a dwelling, because larger numbers will wish to use them. They will accommodate perhaps many groups at one time. The landscape effects as seen by these groups will be studied with certain purposes in mind. The various views themselves as real outdoor pictures will perhaps be the first consideration, but these views should be influenced by the desire of those sitting on the veranda to watch the players in different parts of the course and especially the approach to the 9th and 18th holes. The passing of an island of trees, however, will not detract from the interest, as one can watch the players in approaching the island and a little later as they emerge; a group of foliage in the golf grounds answering the same purpose as an island in a lake.

Perhaps the place for the largest amount of planting would be along the boundaries. The greatest value of the proposed landscape development, however, will not be realized fully unless one takes into account the surrounding land. The development of a successful golf course causes the land along its borders to be much sought after. One can realize the reason for this. Most men in building homes for themselves, if the matter of money did not enter into their calculations, would have fine large places with ample room, the idea perhaps being typified most nearly by a large English estate. If a man can secure an acre or two next to a golf course, the club grounds would form a large part of his estate (Fig. 52). His front yard and broad acres would be mown and taken care of without expense to him save in his annual dues. His domain might, therefore, contain a hundred acres or even more while he would be required to pay taxes on only one or two. A golf club should, therefore, when first looking for grounds, secure if possible all of the land surrounding the proposed area needed for the game, thus providing for future homes for members or others who will appreciate the advantages offered by the exceptional locations. The

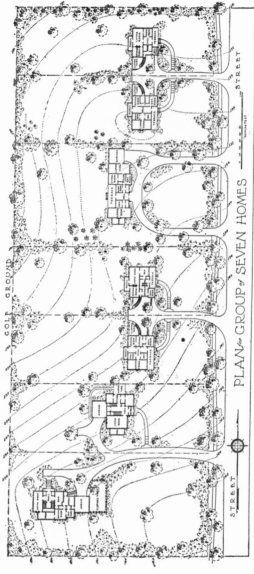

FIG. 52. — THE GOLF GROUNDS. Plan for grounds of seven homes, five of which are on lots 100 feet wide.

ownership of the adjoining land will, moreover, enable the club to control the surroundings so that their future development will not detract from the beauty of the grounds themselves. In some cases, the sale of this additional land for homes has paid the first entire cost of the property. There should not be too many houses or too much evidence of them as seen from the club-house or the points along the course.

With careful study and with planning, the public ground of the course and the private grounds of the surrounding homes can be made to affect each other in such a way as to add to the comfort and the enjoyment of all: to the golf members in the knowledge that no unsightly building will be erected beyond its limits which can injure the appearance of the course, and to those living in the surrounding homes by having the planting done in such a way as to insure them extensive and beautiful views. The selection of location for the homes just mentioned will be in some respects like that of house sites about an attractive lake. In either case, a house can be so placed that its windows will apparently command all the desirable views while the house itself, framed and partly screened by planting, is comparatively inconspicuous.

The grounds of an ideal golf course, ideal from the landscape point of view as well as from the golfer's standpoint, should include not only a good course with extra holes for practice, clock golf, tennis, and perhaps opportunities for other outdoor sports, but it should also contain flower-gardens to furnish flowers for the embellishment of the club-house, and perhaps certain vegetables. With a gardener who had not only technical ability but who was honest and would work for the interest of the club, a large-sized vegetable-garden might be warranted.

Grounds for golf clubs have sometimes been purchased at farm prices and in such cases one can easily imagine that an additional area for a farm, which would be leased to some one who would supply good poultry and dairy products and perhaps wood for the fire-place, might be a wise investment. With many forms of land development, whether for schools, parks, golf grounds, or other public or semi-public use, one naturally reverts to home grounds for a pattern and seeks to introduce many of the features which would make a home attractive. Among such features, a piece of woodland with quantities of wild flowers would be most delightful. A low meadow or bog-garden full of marsh marigolds and bluebells would be charming and in the planting that has been previously mentioned one would look for all those effects which can be found in various parks and especially along the borders of natural woods.

A new game has been described under the name of "arrow golf," which ought to become popular. Like golf, it would make walking interesting. Its arrows, decorated with colored feathers, would be more easily found than golf balls. The bunkers which form the hazards of ordinary golf and are sometimes unsightly would be unnecessary. There would be greater freedom for the exercise of skill in producing beautiful and varied landscape effects. The expense of maintenance should be comparatively small.

In the chapter on Parks, some doubt was expressed as to the propriety of park commissioners allowing portions of the parks under their charge to be used as golf grounds and even going to the expense of developing and maintaining such grounds. Certainly such permission should not be given where the land required is needed by poor people, by great numbers of children, and by men

and women who could not even afford to buy clubs
with which to play.

It is proper to raise the same question as to
whether commissioners having charge of forest
preserves would be justified in taking public land
for golf. If it is proper to take land in the forest
preserve for golf, certainly only that part should be
taken which is vacant, that is naturally without
trees, shrubs, or other attractive growth. If land
in forest preserves is set aside for golf, should it be
developed and maintained at public expense for
the benefit of the comparatively few persons who
would use it? This question need not be discussed
here, but attention is called to the fact that there
can be no objection to golf clubs buying land at
their own expense adjacent to or partly surrounded
by tracts of forest preserve. A juxtaposition of
this kind will be of advantage to both the public
who own the forest and to the golf club. Either
might provide swimming pools, places for coasting,
skating, and playing hockey. Either might occasionally contain a polo field, provided that in the
case of the forest preserve there was no encroach-
ment on the forest. The golf club and the forest
preserve might combine in skating facilities, es-

pecially if there was a lake or river common to both, or they might combine in bridle paths or any other features where they would not interfere with each other. There might, for example, be a path through a woodland border of the golf grounds over which a walking club could route its Saturday afternoon hike without harming any one.

The establishment and use of golf grounds should be encouraged by everyone. Anything which will take persons to the country and give them abundant exercise should be encouraged. Those who cannot afford the time or money to play golf should not envy those who can. The more innocent, healthful enjoyment there can be for a community as a whole, the better. Each individual should feel and acknowledge this whether he himself can or cannot partake in any special form of this enjoyment. If each can form the habit of rejoicing at the happiness of another, it will add to his own comfort and peace of mind.

There is ample land for the production of food. The number of cultivated acres found in the older states might be increased and each acre might produce far more than at present. Let us by all means keep all areas for parks, forest preserves,

golf grounds and all vacant spaces that will contribute to the pleasure and happiness generally.
If clubs will buy and develop such land for the enjoyment of a portion of the community, if they
will pay taxes on it and maintain it without its
being a burden on the public at large, they should
be encouraged to do so.

CHAPTER XV

School Grounds

THE school is the second home of children and its grounds are second only in importance to those of the home itself. They should be given careful consideration, and ample playground should by all means be provided.

IN THE COUNTRY (Fig. 53)

Of all school grounds none is primarily of greater importance than that about a school in the country, and yet none has received less consideration or made less advance toward ideal development.

A story is told of a certain country school. The boys of this school made a practice of going over the fence to an adjoining pasture for the purpose of playing ball. The farmer who owned the pasture complained bitterly to the school-board. There was more or less anger at the boys on the part of both the board and the farmer. Finally, it was

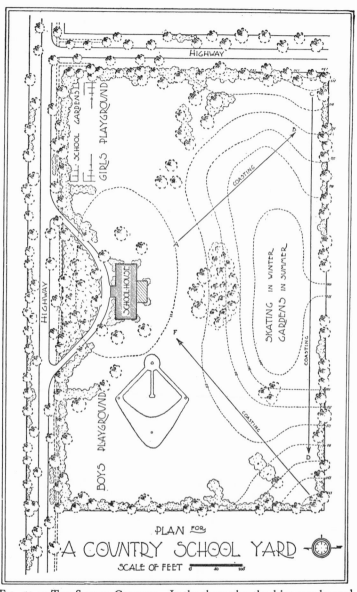

FIG. 53. — THE SCHOOL GROUNDS. In the above plan the drive may be used as a walk and the planting shown may include a variety of trees and shrubs.

decided that all would visit the school together. They arrived during intermission and found the boys in the midst of a game on the forbidden ground. The members of the board became quite interested in the game. At last one bright member asked the farmer what rent he would charge for an acre of land. He replied, naming a very moderate sum which the board at once agreed to pay. The fence was moved to the other side of the acre and all were happy. This incident illustrates that every school should have ample space for play.

There should be room for ball for the girls as well as for the boys, for pull-away and other games, for coasting and skating, for school-gardens and for trees and shrubs that will make the school-house and the grounds attractive in appearance. It would be well if the list of plants included many species so that the plantation would form at least a local arboretum. In selecting the site for a school, all desirable features should be remembered, and advantage taken of any existing hill for coasting if there is one near the proposed site, of existing tree growth, or any feature that will add to the beauty of the ground and to the comfort and entertainment of the pupils. Nor is it the pupils alone that should be considered. There are the teachers and parents. A school in the country is a neighborhood center. Here, from time to time, are various gatherings, usually within the building, but if the grounds are ample and picturesque, they will form an appropriate place for picnics and outdoor meetings of various kinds. Here might be exhibited the products of the school-gardens, or collections of flowers, vegetables and other products of the farms of the neighborhood. The school and its grounds should serve to draw persons together and create a neighborhood spirit which would tend toward improvement in every way. It should lead to greater general intelligence, better crops and more appreciation of beauty.

Naturally, the planting about the ideal school would be arranged along the boundaries, leaving large central open spaces for play and for air and sunlight. Touches of foliage might appear here and there about the building, perhaps from some vines on the walls, some shrubs each side of the entrance steps, or in a reëntrant angle, but there should be nothing to shade the windows. The trees along the boundary might be arranged in groups with spaces left to preserve views or let in breezes. Small trees and shrubs should be used extensively, and there should be an abundance of perennial flowers. The annuals will be taken care of in the gardens for the pupils. An area of five to ten acres would be none too much for this second home for children who usually come from farms of two thousand acres or more. With ten acres, a charming park might be made including within its boundaries a school-house and all the features named.

Higher institutions of learning, including colleges and universities, often take great pains and spend large sums in acquiring and developing beautiful grounds. Such grounds have a great influence on the lives of students. That the love for one's alma mater is often due quite as much to the charm of the campus as to the buildings or the instruction given in them is sometimes claimed by graduates. The influence of an attractive campus extends through life and affects, in a marked degree, the homes built by the alumni. It is important, therefore, to have schools that care for children during the impressionable age from five to fifteen well equipped with beautiful surroundings. Their influence would extend to the homes of the par-

ents as well as to those the children might build
in future years.

It may be said that children will destroy anything
that is planted. This is one reason for planting
school grounds so that youth may be taught to
respect and admire their plant neighbors. Incidentally, certain flowers and portions of plants might
be used with great advantage by the teacher in giving instruction in botany, not in classes, but in
general talks that would interest and give recreation. Such short talks on natural objects or phe-
nomena which pupils can observe for themselves
are often restful, because they introduce variety
and give instruction that can be "soaked in" by
the students without apparent effort or responsibility on their part.

IN CITIES

It would be well if many of the features of country schools could be retained in the city. The school
in the city should have ample grounds and should
continue to be a neighborhood center. There
should be space for play and for trees without shut-
ting out light. Perhaps the play might be concentrated more than in the country by using swings,

slides, and other apparatus, but even then there should be abundant room for gardens, borders of shrubs, skating, and coasting. If school grounds could be planned in advance before the property needed is covered with expensive buildings, they could be developed with far greater economy than under present methods. Since school-houses have often been erected in cities on small sites allowing no room for outdoor exercise, it has fallen to the lot of various public-spirited bodies, including boards of aldermen, park commissions and improvement associations, to supply playgrounds. This causes much duplication of effort and expenditure of time and money that would have been unnecessary with the exercise of wise foresight.

Now that city planning is receiving attention, perhaps future school yards will become adequate. In general, they should contain all the features found in the best playgrounds. There should be room for tennis, baseball, and other games, for gymnastic apparatus, and provision for swimming, space for trees to give shade and make the grounds attractive, and there should be shrubs and flowers. The grounds should be planned so that portions of them could be flooded in winter for skating.

The space allotted for a school ground should be sufficient for a combination of what is usually found at present in a typical school yard, playground, and small park. The cost of the original investment and the maintenance of such a combination would be much less than that of separate areas under different managements, while the accommodation would be far greater for play, for neighborhood gatherings, and for everything tending to unite and improve the community tributary to the school. Such an institution, providing facilities for education and recreation, would bring together teachers, children and parents and create a healthful, stimulating neighborhood spirit that is now generally lacking.

CHAPTER XVI

Arboretums and Botanic Gardens

The most satisfactory and useful planting project in the United States is the Arnold Arboretum at Boston. It gathers its material from all temperate regions. It issues bulletins regarding not only the trees and shrubs of the United States and Canada but also those that are available from different parts of Europe and Asia. At the Arboretum one can actually see and study the individual trees and shrubs mentioned in the bulletins and in many cases study their effects in groups or masses. If one can visit the Arboretum at different seasons of the year, one can observe the winter effects of branching, the appearance of buds and leaves, the blossoms, the summer foliage, the autumn coloring and the fruits of hundreds of species of woody growth.

While the development of the Arnold Arboretum has been admirable, it is seen by only a small fraction of those who should learn the facts which it can teach, a small part even of those who are interested in landscape-gardening. The United States is so vast in extent, it has so many variations of soil and climate and its people live so far apart that it should have more than one arboretum. Other experiment stations and government plantations in various sections of the United States are doing good work, but more arboretums devoted especially to planting material suitable for landscape work are greatly needed. There should be at least a great comprehensive arboretum for the central northern part of the United States, one or more for each of those sections known as the Rocky Mountain region, the coast and the southern states. Even with arboretums in the localities named, these should be supplemented by plantations at universities, especially where landscape-gardening is taught, and in the parks of the various cities. An individual who wishes to develop beautiful home grounds should be able to see and become acquainted with the available planting material for this purpose in the parks of any neighboring city. In the latter especially, one should have an opportunity of judging the effects of different trees and shrubs in landscape work. For their educational value, labels giving names, localities and dates of planting would be very useful.

In an arboretum, the space allotted to each plant or group of plants should be large enough to allow full development for each individual or group and also open surrounding space so that trees and shrubs can be seen to advantage even when they have reached old age and attained their greatest size. The land selected for an arboretum should, if possible, have a varied topography with slopes to the north, south, east and west and each plant should be placed in its most appropriate location in regard to slope, soil, and moisture. For example, birches and hemlocks should be on the north slope. Most trees and shrubs noted for their blossoms should have a south or at least a sunny exposure. Some trees prefer sand or gravel and others a clay soil.

The roads and walks in the arboretum should be planned with easy lines and grades with the plants to be seen from them so placed that they can be observed conveniently. To save space and expense, there should be comparatively few roads. Those who are studying plants can do so best when walking or standing.

Even though an arboretum is primarily a museum,

its plans should be influenced by a desire to produce pleasing landscape effects. A hillside showing at different seasons the flowers of sugar maples, june-berries, red-buds, dogwoods, crab-apples and haw-thorns can be planted so as to show beautiful pictures as well as the characteristics of the different plants. Evergreens can be planted so as to show the characteristic development of the individuals with branches spreading out and resting upon the ground and also in time showing the group and trunk effects as seen in their native forests. Community effects with trees and shrubs that grow naturally as neighbors can also be shown. An ideal arboretum would require a large area, but as it is for the benefit of a wide section of country the necessary space should be provided.

An arboretum should serve not only for the study of the plants it contains but to some extent at least as a public park. It should have beautiful scenery with hills and valleys and at the bottom of the latter either running streams or reflections from smooth surfaces of water, supplemented by open glades of lawn or meadow.

It will be advantageous if the site chosen for an arboretum contains some native forest growth with full-sized trees as well as younger ones and a varied growth of small trees and shrubs. Such a forest with plenty of adjacent open space will make a good background for various plantations and will help out in the landscape effects mentioned in the preceding paragraph. It will also illustrate the variety, gracefulness, and picturesqueness of nature and this will tend to improve the character of the artificial plantations. It cannot too frequently be realized that nature is the best teacher and that even in the museum-like arboretum she can give points on arrangement.

The arboretums thus far discussed have been of large areas intended for giving pleasure and instruction to the residents of many states, but there is no reason why cities, villages, townships, even individual estates, should not have smaller arboretums for local study. Every park commission, cemetery association, or body having charge of public grounds of any kind should continually make collections and try experiments. A farmer's family could obtain great pleasure by experimenting with different ornamental trees, shrubs, and flowers as well as those planted primarily for fruit. Such collections and experiments wherever land is devoted to tree growth,

although not as comprehensive as those connected
with great arboretums, will nevertheless be seen by
many persons who have not time to travel far from
their own homes and will lead to that ideal enjoyment in life that accompanies an acquaintance with
the beauties of nature.

BOTANIC GARDENS

Supplementing the arboretums, there should be
botanic gardens. Such gardens exist in many places.
The Kew Gardens at London, the Jardin des Plantes
at Paris, and the New York Botanic Garden in the
Bronx may be mentioned as examples. There are
many smaller gardens and these should be even more
numerous than the smaller arboretums that have
been mentioned. Many schemes might be followed
in designing a botanic garden. It might be arranged
to show the native flora, each plant being seen in
its favorite situation as to soil, shade, and moisture
and accompanied by its usual neighbors. It might
be planted to represent all hardy herbaceous plants,
those that are introduced as well as indigenous. It
might be arranged with regard to classification, all
the leguminous plants being in one locality, all with
composite flowers in another, and so on. There

might be gardens showing the sequence of bloom from early spring to late fall. A comprehensive botanic garden should contain somewhere a collection of medicinal plants, of plants noted for their perfume, a bog-garden, and plants arranged with regard to the color of their flowers.

There is hardly any limit to the number of ideas that can be followed in designing a botanic garden. No artificial scheme, however, can be quite as satisfactory to the botanist as nature's own garden when left undisturbed. A botanist likes to go to an unfrequented marsh, or a bit of woods, a meadow, the margin of a lake, or a hedge row. No botanic garden is ever more interesting than the more or less open woods on the back end of a farm, containing perhaps a stream supplemented by pools of water occupying its abandoned channels in which water-lilies and various water plants are growing; woods protecting shade-loving flowers; woods filled with openings of moist soil, where many kinds of ferns will find a congenial home; woods including sunny sandy ridges for lupines, puccoon, spiderwort and various graceful grasses; woods having some evergreens and larches with moist partially shaded situations beloved by lady-slippers and ladies' tresses.

Such a situation, combining tree and shrub growth with that of herbaceous plants, containing an abundance of shade and sun, leading the botanist on from one interesting plant to another, keeping him more or less excited over the prospect of making new discoveries, is the ideal one for a botanic garden.

Such gardens of more or less limited extent might exist on almost every farm, or even in the home grounds of suburbs. The designer of a large public botanic garden should certainly be influenced in making his plans by a recollection of the favorite haunts of botany students and collectors. Public gardens must of course have walks for visitors, but they might be surrounded by wooded plantations which would give a charming seclusion and protection from wind. They might have the charm of varied outlines and variety of soils and situations to suit the tastes of different plants and combine an artistic arrangement with the utilitarian object of affording a chance for study.

There would be some advantage in combining a botanic garden, arboretum, and forest preserve, since each would supplement the other. The background of a forest of considerable extent would give a charm to both the arboretum and the garden. The former might be irregular in outline. Perhaps it might cover a series of ridges or hills and its borders might form numerous projections and bays of large extent, giving ideal situations for additional plants. Trees, shrubs, and flowers are growing together in nature and it is, therefore, fitting that they should be associated in plantations made by man.

U

CHAPTER XVII

Cemeteries

THE cemeteries of the present day that are located in the suburbs of large cities came into existence from a desire to have burials at a distance from the centers of population and in places with beautiful surroundings. They are often called "rural cemeteries." The first one in the United States to merit this name was Mt. Auburn, near Boston, Massachusetts, founded in 1831. Since then the idea of having burial places park-like in their character has been spreading until they contain today some of the most beautiful landscapes developed by the hand of man. The wish to have in the cemetery the beauty of trees, shrubs, lawns, and flowers has gradually led to the abolition of fences, coping, and other lot inclosures, and a reduction in the number of monuments and the size of headstones (Fig. 54). Many persons now believe that the last resting-place should be surrounded by the quietness and beauty of these features of nature's

Fig. 54. — The Cemetery Landscape. Typical burial lots, trees, and monuments. The shadows from near-by trees indicate the grade of the lawn.

handiwork without distracting stonework or artificial objects. Others say that "the cemetery should be a cemetery," meaning by this that it should resemble somewhat closely the old conventional churchyard or graveyard, with its multitude of crowded tombstones inscribed with the good qualities of those buried within its walls.

All agree that the cemetery should be so situated and maintained as to menace in no way the healthfulness of surrounding neighborhoods, but, as conducted at present, no areas are freer from contagion or do less to pollute the atmosphere than those devoted to burials. Cemeteries, indeed, rank with parks in preserving open spaces and in the growth of foliage which purifies the air. The ideal location is one where the ground is somewhat undulating and thoroughly drained by having a porous subsoil, while the surface soil is sufficiently rich and deep to support a good growth of vegetation. In some instances, as at Forest Hills, Boston, and at Woodlawn, New York, it has been necessary to blast and remove rock and then fill in the space with earth. In other cases, the natural soil has been so poor that it has been necessary to cover it with a rich earth hauled from a long distance. In still other cases it has been necessary to select a clay soil because there was no other, or to make ground by excavating lakes, using the material excavated to raise the surrounding land, or to inter above ground in structures erected for the purpose, as at New Orleans.

SUBDIVISIONS, WALKS, AND DRIVES (Fig. 55)

When a site is chosen, it is usually subdivided into sections and lots, which must be made accessible by the construction of drives and walks. A road should pass within about 150 feet of every lot. The width of the roadways should vary according to the size of the cemetery and the probable amount of driving. If the area is very small, a drive may be unnecessary. As cemeteries increase in size, a grass walk eight feet in width may answer every purpose, using this when needed as a drive; then a driveway sixteen feet in width may be required in a somewhat larger area so that vehicles can pass each other; and, finally, a cemetery designed to accommodate large populations should have good roadways, usually twenty-four feet in width. Formerly these roadways would have been constructed of ordinary macadam or gravel, but with the increased use of automobiles, the material used for roadways should be bitulithic con-

Fig. 55. — The Picture in the Cemetery. A cemetery drive framed by an old willow.

crete, bitulithic macadam, cement concrete, or brick, preference being given to the first.

Walks should usually be left in grass and form part of a continuous lawn, being of better appearance and more easily maintained than those of gravel. The location of the drives will determine the shapes and sizes of the sections, the ideal size being from 250 to 300 feet in width and 700 or 800 feet in length. The plan should be made after a careful study of the ground in question, the drives being placed so they will have easy grades, command good views and be as few as possible when spaced approximately 300 feet apart. When the ground is irregular in shape, undulating or hilly, or contains streams or lakes or valuable trees, these features may make it necessary to vary somewhat from the directions just given. After the general scheme has been studied out in connection with a topographical survey of the land selected, the roads can be staked out on the ground by eye with better effect than if drawn first in an office. They should nearly always be curved to produce the most pleasing result, a curved drive-way being advisable because: (1) when the margins are properly planted, certain portions of the ground are always hidden, thus becoming more interesting;

(2) they insure varied effects of light and shade; (3) they make the average distance from the cemetery entrance to the lots shorter than if one follows straight lines and turns right angles.

An open tract, to begin with, is in many ways preferable to one that is thickly wooded, but groups of trees or single specimens that have broadened out in a natural way would be very valuable, since they would help to take away the naked, forbidding appearance of land newly planted with young trees. On a vacant area, it is usually advisable to plant some large trees for the sake of immediate effect. These can be grouped about the entrance, a fork in the drives, the top of a hill, the margin of a lake, or other distinguishing position. The objection to a piece of land covered with thick woods is that the necessary thinning to secure sufficient open space will leave tall spindling trees, unused to exposure. These are not very attractive in themselves, are very likely to die, and are liable to be blown down. If there are thick woods in the land selected, the trees chosen to remain should be those that are healthiest and have the lowest branches. Occasionally, the trees removed may be cut off at the ground so that sprouts will spring from the roots and form beautiful bush-like specimens.

BUILDINGS AND PLANTING

The necessary buildings will vary with the size of the cemetery, but they should always be modest in appearance and suitably embellished with shrubbery and vines. The office would naturally be placed near the entrance to avoid unnecessary walking, but it should not be built immediately on the highway or public street (Fig. 56). The large stone or brick arch frequently over the gateway is usually too pretentious in appearance and not in keeping with the character of the grounds. A natural archway of living trees would be better. The chapel, if any, should be placed some distance within the grounds to give it greater seclusion and quietness.

Whether there should be greenhouses or not is a question that should be answered in accordance with local conditions. It may merely be said that with the great variety of flowering trees and shrubs available, as well as the thousands of hardy flowering herbaceous plants, most beautiful effects can be produced without the expense, the continual labor and the bare beds for more than half the year, which go with the construction of greenhouses and the use of bedding plants. Frequently, many of the trees,

FIG. 56. — A CEMETERY ENTRANCE.   A pleasing combination of architecture and planting.

shrubs, and herbaceous plants needed may be found in the adjacent country. Thus, elms, maples, lindens, viburnums, and dogwoods may be moved from the edges of farm wood-lots and produce almost immediately an effect of age and beauty. To prevent intrusion, a fence along the boundary of a cemetery is necessary. This can be of wire hidden by a belt of trees and shrubbery, or it can be a substantial wall (Fig. 57).

No one would now make the cemetery dreary by confining the planting to spruces and weeping willows. On the contrary, every effort is devoted to securing bright cheerful effects by the selection of all kinds of flowering happy-looking plants. The modern cemetery becomes, in fact, a sort of arboretum. It includes some evergreens which are most suitably grouped along the boundary belt, and which should contain all kinds of hardy pines, as well as some of the more stiff and formal spruces and cedars. The planting of Norway spruces has in many places been overdone. The development of attractive landscapes in cemeteries is of so much importance that Mr. Strauch, the greatest cemetery designer whom we have had, used to call the present method "the landscape lawn plan."

Fig. 57.— A Cemetery Boundary from the Outside. It is placed five or six feet inside of the boundary line to give room for planting. While a wall of this kind gives a desirable seclusion, it need not be bare and forbidding or prison-like in appearance as seen from a street.

RULES FOR MAINTAINING CEMETERIES

A landscape in the cemetery should improve with years of growth. It must first be intelligently designed, and then receive care and attention from someone familiar and in sympathy with the scheme adopted. To insure such attention, and to protect the interest of all lot-owners, as well as to maintain the dignity and character of a city of the dead, rules have been adopted by all leading cemeteries. These are the result of study and experience on the part of many men. At a meeting of the Association of American Cemetery Superintendents, held at Boston, in 1890, the following rules were recommended by a unanimous vote of those in attendance:

RULE 1. (This should be a general rule, stating the authority and conditions on which lots are sold and the restrictions on transfers. The rule, of course, would have to be varied according to conditions existing in each cemetery.)

RULE 2. The trustees desire to leave the improvement of lots, as far as possible, to the taste of the owners; but, in justice to all, they reserve the right, given them by law, to exclude or remove from any lot any headstone, monument or other structure, tree, plant, or other object whatever which may conflict with the regulations, or which they shall consider injurious to the general appearance of the grounds; but no trees growing within any lot shall be removed or trimmed without the consent of the trustees.

RULE 3. Lot-owners may have planting or other work done on their lots at their expense, upon application to the superintendent. No workmen other than employees of the cemetery will be admitted to the cemetery except for the purpose of setting stonework.

RULE 4. No iron or wire-work and no seats or vases will be allowed on lots, excepting by permission of the trustees, and when any article made of iron begins to rust the same shall be removed from the cemetery.

RULE 5. The trustees desire to encourage the planting of trees and shrubbery, but, in order to protect the rights of all and to secure the best general results, they require that such planting shall be done only in accordance with the directions of the superintendent of the cemetery.

RULE 6. No coping nor any kind of inclosure will be permitted. The boundaries of lots will be marked by corner-stones, which will be set by the cemetery, at the expense of the lot-owner, with the centers upon the lines bounding the lot. Corner-stones must not project above the ground and must not be altered nor removed.

RULE 7. No lots shall be filled above the established grade.

RULE 8. All interments in lots shall be restricted to the members of the family or relations of the lot-owner.

RULE 9. No disinterment will be allowed without the permission of the trustees, of the lot-owner, and of the next of kin of the deceased.

RULE 10. Mounds over graves should be kept low, not exceeding four inches in height; and stone or other inclosures around graves will not be allowed.

RULE 11. Foundations for all monuments, headstones, and the like, shall be built by the cemetery at the expense of the lot-owner and fifteen days' notice must be given for the building of foundations. The cost of the same must be paid in advance.

RULE 12. Every foundation must be at least as wide and as long as the base stone resting upon it, and must not project above the surface of the ground. All foundations must extend as low as the bottom of the grave.

RULE 13. Only one monument will be permitted on a family burial-lot.

RULE 14. (This should be a rule limiting the height of the headstones, and the lower this limit is made the better. Even with the lawn is considered best.)

RULE 15. All stone and marble works, monuments and headstones, must be accepted by the superintendent as being in conformity with the foregoing rules before being taken into the cemetery.

RULE 16. No monument, headstone or coping, and no portion of any vault above ground shall be constructed of other material than cut stone or real bronze. No artificial material will be permitted.

RULE 17. The trustees wish, as far as possible, to discourage the building of vaults, believing, with the best landscape-gardeners of the day, that they are generally injurious to the appearance of the grounds, and, unless constructed with great care, are apt to leak and are liable to rapid decay, and in course of time to become unsightly ruins. Therefore no vaults will be permitted to be built unless the designs for the same are exceptionally good, and the construction is solid and thorough. The designs must be submitted to the trustees, and will not be approved unless the structure would, in their judgment, be an architectural ornament to the cemetery.

RULE 18. Material for stone or marble work will not be allowed to remain in the cemetery longer than shall be strictly necessary, and refuse or unused material must be removed as soon as the work is completed. In case of neglect, such removal will be made by the cemetery at the expense of the lot-owner and contractor, who shall be severally responsible. No material of any kind will be received at the cemetery after 12 o'clock M. on Saturdays.

RULE 19. The trustees shall have the right to make exceptions from the foregoing rules in favor of designs which they consider exceptionally artistic and ornamental, and such exceptions shall not be construed as a rescission of any rule.

RULE 20. It shall be the duty and right of the trustees from time to time to lay out and alter such avenues and walks, and to make such rules and regulations for the government of the grounds as they may deem requisite and proper and calculated to secure and promote the general object of the cemetery.

RULE 21. The superintendent is directed to enforce the above regulations and to exclude from the cemetery any person willfully violating the same.

Cemeteries should be established on a basis to enable those in authority to take uniform care of the grounds for all time. The prices charged for lots should be high enough to enable a fund to be set aside that will yield an annual income sufficient to pay all necessary general expenses. In laying out a new cemetery, those in charge should seek the best advice available. Such advice should be based on a thorough knowledge of landscape-gardening and the special needs of burial-grounds. Much information can be obtained by visiting Spring Grove, at Cincinnati, Ohio, generally recognized as the

Fig. 58. — The Nobility of Trees and Background. A tomb with a satisfactory setting, and simple in all its details.

x

pioneer of park-like cemeteries, and perhaps the best example in the world. Oakwoods Cemetery at Troy, New York, Swan Point at Providence, Rhode Island, and Forest Hills at Boston are prominent examples of landscape cemeteries. Graceland at Chicago, although smaller in area than those already mentioned, contains some good landscape effects. Many other cemeteries in the vicinity of the large cities of the United States can be commended on account of the good taste displayed in them. There are others which, while containing many beautiful trees and expensive monuments, include also many fences, railings, copings, and hedges that serve as examples of what to avoid rather than to imitate.

The leading cemeteries should keep pace with the best thought of the times, with the best theories of religion, science, and economics. They should be, as the name implies, sleeping-places, places of rest and freedom from intrusion. It seems natural that one should seek for such a place the very best production of landscape-art, where spreading lawns give a cheerful sunny effect; where pleasing vistas show distant clouds or the setting sun; where branching trees give grateful shade (Fig. 58), furnish pleasing objects to look at, and places for birds to come each year and sing again their welcome songs; where blossoming shrubs delight the eye, perfume the air, and make attractive nesting-places. Such features may seem to exist more for the living than for the dead, but the living are the ones that need them. If it seems natural to choose a beautiful park for a sleeping-place, it seems incongruous to put into this picture obelisk after obelisk, stone posts and slabs of all shapes and sizes, and stone tombs.

The problem presented to cemetery associations is how to secure the most pleasing combinations of growing plants, including trees, shrubs, flowers, and grass, the most satisfactory views, the most harmonious and restful park, for the cemetery is really a memorial park.

COUNTRY CEMETERIES

Often a country cemetery has a most forlorn and neglected appearance, being merely a combination of monuments and headstones, uncut grass, Irish junipers and spruces. This appearance is not due so much to lack of money as to sparsity of ideas. The cost of the monuments shows there has been money to spend, but there has not been an appreciation of beauty. In one neglected country cemetery, a beautiful ground-covering of a little euphorbia had killed out the grass. It was far better-looking than the uncut grass-covered areas, yet a farmer regretted its existence. Other areas were covered with myrtle (*Vinca minor*) and were always green and beautiful. Where it is not feasible to mow and water grass, the selection of various ground-covering plants, like those named, would serve well in its place. Partridge-berry, trailing juniper, bugle, Japanese spurge, lily-of-the-valley, two-leaved Solomon's seal, butter-and-eggs, wild violets, erythroniums, hepaticas, and many other plants, serve well for a ground cover, some thriving in shade and others in the sun (Fig. 59).

With the growth of an appreciation of beautiful landscapes and planting effects in connection with homes, school grounds and highways, it is but natural that there should develop a country cemetery far more beautiful than any seen at present.

Fig. 59. — The Garden in the Cemetery. Tulips under an oak.

CHAPTER XVIII

City and Regional Planning

A new line of endeavor has appeared in the United States in recent years, known usually as city planning, but sometimes as city and regional planning. It has been undertaken by landscape-designers, architects, and engineers working individually or in conjunction. "Zoning" is intimately connected with city planning, but may be applied to cities that have already been planned and built or built without planning. Nearly all American cities have just grown by "additions." These have usually been planned in surveyors' offices without any consideration of the topography. A ravine or a hill has been divided into lots as though it were level ground.

If it is worth while to plan a house, spending much time in studying the arrangement of the rooms, the location and size of windows and other details, and the fitting of the house to its proposed site, or to plan a school-house or a factory, it is certainly worth while to spend much time in planning a city which will contain perhaps thousands of buildings and which will outlast a long series of structures erected upon the same site. The city plan should be studied with reference to the hills and valleys when these are found within its boundaries; with regard to the location of factories, warehouses, shops, residences, apartment buildings, offices, stores and public buildings, allowing room for the probable growth in each class of buildings; studying it with reference to its connection with the surrounding country by means of the various highways, and also with reference to those localities not especially adapted to any of the purposes named, but very useful as parks, open spaces, forests, water views and glimpses into the open spaces outside of the city. Intelligent study with reference to the locations of the different classes of buildings and the streets and parks would have saved vast sums in construction and maintenance, and, what is of even more importance, would have preserved and developed the beauty of cities. The fundamental beauty of a city, which depends on its arrangement of streets and its preservation of hills, valleys, streams, rivers, and lakes in all their natural loveliness, lasts for generations.

The citizens of a city that is wisely planned for the preservation and development of its beauty do not leave it to go to other more attractive cities when they have acquired a competence. When they travel, no matter how far, they come back with the feeling that they are glad to get home. A common remark on such occasions is, "This city looks good to me. I am willing to live and die right here."

It is this feeling of pride in one's own town or neighborhood, a feeling that one is identified with it, is, in fact, a part of it, and, in a measure, responsible for it, that is important. This feeling of identification with one's surroundings should extend from the city to the country and from the country to the city; a farmer thinking of the neighboring town as being, to a certain extent, his, and the dweller in the city having a corresponding feeling with regard to the country. Each should try to help the other.

The city planner, therefore, should take into consideration the mutual dependence of the city and country on each other and design a territory immediately outside of the city limits. This has long been the custom in England, where planning commissions have control of the location of new streets far beyond city boundaries.

When city planning was first discussed in America, the subject most frequently mentioned was "civic centers." By this was meant an orderly convenient arrangement of the post-office, city-hall, court-house, and other public buildings with regard to each other and to the remainder of the city, of which the group named would form the heart or center.

Usually, however, American cities that have received treatment at the hands of city planners are already blessed with city-halls and the other public buildings naturally associated with civic centers. To make changes regarding them would be very expensive, and, usually, even if such changes are deemed advisable, they can be made as well at some future time. In the outskirts of a city, however, where it is growing, the need for wise planning is urgent, since delay here may prevent forever the adoption of the best locations for streets or the best regulations for the development of the land. It is here that there may still be a chance to save a stream, a wooded hillside, an Indian mound, or other historic or natural feature. It is here that the change in the location of a street may save expense in construction and forever add to the beauty and convenience of the lots on either side. It is here that suitable areas may be saved for residences, factories, school-houses, parks, churches, and all the different classes of buildings or spaces that will be required in the city.

While city planning, which takes into account the probable growth of a city, the requirements of all its different kinds of business and residences, its schools and other public buildings, its parks and playgrounds and its connection with the country and other cities, is comparatively new in this country, landscape-gardeners have long been called on to plan suburbs or villages, or special areas, called subdivisions or allotments.

Clifton and Walnut Hills of Cincinnati, and Lake Forest and Riverside near Chicago, may be cited as examples. The planning of such areas has usually been primarily for residences, although, sometimes, sites for school-houses and churches have been designated. Those qualifications which would fit a man for planning intelligently home grounds would naturally qualify him for laying out a collection of such grounds. It is in the outskirts of a town, the places where homes are being developed, that the services of a landscape-gardener are especially needed.

The steps to be taken in planning a subdivision

may be mentioned in the order in which they should be taken.

(1) A visit to the property and a talk with its owner and the city authorities regarding proper sizes of lots, width of streets, probable requirements for school grounds, parks and other public needs. Some cities now require that a certain percentage of the land be set aside for parks or playgrounds. While such a provision is better than none, it would not always result in choosing land that is best adapted to park purposes.

(2) Assuming that the general problems mentioned in (1) are satisfactorily settled so that the only questions remaining are those of actually planning for streets and lots, the next step would be the preparation of a plat based on a topographical survey. Such a plat should show the lie of the land by contour lines, the contour interval depending somewhat on the nature of the land and the character of the proposed development. Usually, it is from one to five feet. The contour intervals should be uniform so that the contours will indicate at a glance the relative steepness of the surface in different parts of the property. They would show at once the location of ravines and other inequalities.

The plat should also indicate bodies of water, rock ledges, outlines of woods, and special trees or other objects which can be determined easily and definitely. With such a plat in hand, the landscape-gardener should be able promptly to locate his position upon it while studying the land itself. The topographical plat can be made by the landscape-gardener or someone from his office, or by a surveyor. In making the survey, the stadia method is the most economical and the best. Dividing the land up into squares with stakes at the corners is useful for some purposes, but generally the stakes are lost so that it is difficult, without going over the work of surveying a second time, to find one's location on the property. The making of a topographical survey by means of squares is slow and expensive. It is always a satisfaction, when looking at a topographical plat and seeing some special object like a big rock, a thirty-inch sycamore tree, or a spring, to be able to look on the land itself and see definitely the object indicated. It is unsatisfactory to find on the plat a special object, like a twelve-inch black oak, and discover on the land a dozen such oaks near the location designated, any one of which might be the tree that had been surveyed. Either all the trees should be indicated as accurately as possible, or the one shown must be so distinct from the others that there will be no question as to its identity.

(3) With the topographical plat in hand, the landscape-gardener can soon decide on a general scheme of subdivision which he would recommend to the owner of the property, and this can be sketched on a print of the survey and then discussed with all parties interested.

(4) As soon as the plan is agreed on, either as sketched, or with such modifications as may be adopted, it is advisable actually to stake out the center lines of proposed streets by the method described under Home Grounds (see page 128). The reason for staking the center line of a proposed street upon the ground before definitely drawing it on a plat is that by so doing it will more accurately fit the land and be more pleasing in its curves. A curve drawn on a plat will usually appear too pronounced on the ground, because, in the latter case, it will in appearance be very much foreshortened. Other reasons for staking the line on the ground first are: (a) The valuable trees or shrubs may be saved or left in such positions that they will be effective with regard to the proposed street; (b) advantage may

be taken of fine views which would not be appreciated when merely looking at a plat; (c) the topography itself will be better appreciated when seen full size than when drawn to a scale which must necessarily be small.

(5) With the center lines of streets staked on the land, these lines can be surveyed and shown accurately on a plat. The plat should indicate the curved lines by offsets from the sides of a polygon whose angles and sides lie within the boundary lines of the proposed streets. It is a great mistake to require that the curves shall be arcs of circles as in the case of railroads. Often a good curve has been spoiled by attempting to make it fit this requirement.

(6) With streets definitely located, the next step in the preparation of a plat is the subdivision of the property into lots. If the land is vacant and comparatively level and featureless, this work can be done in an office, but if there are existing trees, great variation of surfaces, rocky ledges or attractive views, it is advisable actually to go on the land, select a site for each house, putting in a stake at what would be its approximate center, and then locate these stakes and put them on the plat. This method will

enable one to picture in his mind the appearance of the land when occupied by houses. He will know that a desirable view, as seen from one house, will not be cut off by the construction of houses on other lots. Planning in this way will insure for the future residents of the subdivision in question as great advantages as should be derived by all the dwellers of a city from careful city planning.

(7) Having finally made a plan showing streets and lots, with locations for houses, other plats can be made showing pavements, sidewalks, profiles of streets, cross-sections, methods of surface drainage, and location of planting. In staking out the streets, the designer has naturally in mind the grades to be adopted, and has tested these by means of a hand level to ascertain that a grade within the adopted limits is feasible. If there are existing trees on the land that is being studied, these will be taken into consideration in preparing a planting plan and also in fixing the profiles of roadways. Often, by changing the grade of a roadway slightly from that which would naturally be adopted on entirely vacant land, a good tree standing in the parkway can be saved, and it is usually possible to change the grade without making the road too steep or the profile unpleasant.

The planting plan will show existing growth, especially along the street borders, and also the trees and shrubs that are to be planted. With large lots, in addition to showing the site for the house, it is often advisable to indicate the proper location for the entrance drive and the garage and perhaps some suggestion of the arrangement of open spaces about the house.

The chapters on plant materials, planting arrangement, and thoroughfares contain information applicable to the planting plans for subdivisions.

The cost of grading and making other improvements in a subdivision planned in accordance with the directions given in this chapter should be relatively small, that is, much less than by ordinary methods, while the beauty of an area developed along the natural lines described would give pleasure to generations yet to come.

APPENDIX

Two papers by the late Bryan Lathrop (1844–1916), president of Graceland Cemetery Co., trustee of estates and of the Art Institute of Chicago, patron of literature and art, president of the Chicago Orchestral Association.

A PLEA FOR LANDSCAPE-GARDENING

THE intelligent traveler observes one very striking difference between Europe and America.

In Europe he sees almost everywhere evidences of a sense of beauty. In America, almost everywhere he is struck by the want of it. In Europe, and in Asia too, the work of man adds to the beauty of the picturesqueness of scenery. In America, it usually makes a blot upon it. I do not conclude from this that the American people have no sense of beauty, but only that in the mass it has not been cultivated. The mass is ignorant of beauty. In this new country of ours the struggle for existence has been intense, and the practical side of life has been developed while the æsthetic side has lain dormant.

To awaken this great nation to a love of the beauties of nature is, therefore, a mission of the first importance, and the time is ripe for the work. Signs of awakening are to be seen on every side, but much depends on the direction to be given to these new impulses of a people still in the main groping in the dark. Where shall we look for this direction? Obviously, I think, to Landscape-Gardening.

Landscape-Gardening is one of the rarest and greatest of the fine arts, but the one which has been least understood or appreciated. If it is an art to paint a landscape on a small canvas with brushes and paints, is it less an art to make a picture on broad acres, using for material God's own earth, grass, trees, shrubs, and flowers? As a nation we have yet to learn that such an art exists.

Only last year when I suggested taking the advice of a highly trained landscape-gardener, one of the most intelligent women of my acquaintance asked me if "any one could not plant a tree?" Any one can build a house, but is the result good architecture? Any one can apply paint to a canvas, but is the result a pleasing picture?

Landscape-Gardening is not only one of the noblest of the fine arts, but in its perfection it is one of the most difficult.

When the architect, the painter, and the sculptor have done their work it is as complete and perfect as the artist can make it. Not so with the landscape-gardener. He must plant with the eye of a prophet, for it requires many years to bring to perfection the picture which he has imagined. He must know the character of every tree and shrub, the size, shape, and color which it will have at maturity.

If he has designed his landscape with prophetic skill, it will grow in beauty year by year, intensifying the varieties of surface, creating vistas in which imagination delights; the masses of trees and shrubs will have assumed pyramidal form, contrasting or harmonizing each with the other; and the nature foliage will have acquired that exquisite blending of tones which is the despair of the painter.

The ideal landscape-gardener should have a vast range of knowledge. He must be a botanist, and he must know the nature, the habits of growth, of trees, shrubs, and plants, and those which are adapted to each region; he should know the chemistry of horticulture, and the nature of soils; he should be an engineer, as the basis of his work is the grading and shaping of the earth's surface; he should have a knowledge of architecture, as his work will often make or mar the work of the architect; and finally he must be an artist to the tips of his fingers; the more artistic he is the better landscape-gardener he will be.

His life is devoted to a reverent and loving study of the most beautiful effects of nature and to the work of reproducing them for the pleasure of man.

My conclusion, then, is that we must look to landscape-gardening for our inspiration in the new gospel of natural beauty. It will teach us how a background of trees and a few vines trained by loving hands will transform the baldest cottage into a charming feature of a landscape.

The wild growth along a country roadside may be as lovely as anything painted by Rousseau. Let us teach the farmer to see its beauty and to leave it untouched.

The Women's Clubs have undertaken a noble work in teaching the people to see and to love beautiful things. May their efforts be crowned with success. May they redeem our country from the curse of bare and bald ugliness in the work of man. May the time come soon when our streets shall be lined with trees and shrubs; when front yards, and back yards too, shall be softened by masses of flowering shrubs; and when the farmhouses, the cottages, and the factories along our railways shall be redeemed by spreading trees and by shrubbery and creeping vines; when the European traveler in this country may be as much delighted by its beauty as he is now impressed by its prosperity.

PARKS AND LANDSCAPE-GARDENING

A paper read at the Boston meeting of the American Park and Outdoor Art Association

My first experience as a park commissioner was a surprise and a shock.

For about eight years Lincoln Park had been given over to the politicians, with the usual result, — extravagance, mismanagement, neglect and decay. The new board of commissioners was pledged to the reformation of abuses and the restoration of the park. Our success depended upon securing a man eminently qualified to be superintendent. He was to take the place once filled so ably by Mr. Pettigrew, who now has charge of the model park system of this country. We were deluged with letters recommending for superintendent a very estimable gentleman, a retired quartermaster of the United States army, who had every qualification for the office except one; he knew nothing of the making and care of parks; nothing of soils and fertilizers; of artistic grading; of planting and pruning; of the maintenance of lawns; of the nature and habits of trees and shrubs, or the effect of time on their form and color in masses; in short, he had no knowledge of even the rudimentary principles of landscape-gardening. The letters of recommendation came from presidents of railways and of banks, and leading men of affairs and in the learned professions; and in all these letters there was not one word about landscape-gardening or a suggestion that any knowledge of it is a requisite in the management of parks.

It was this that surprised and shocked me.

The writers of them are fairly representative of the country at large, since it is well known that few men of middle age in Chicago were born or brought up there. Let us consider for a moment what a park should be.

The true function of a park is to afford a refuge to the dwellers in cities where they may escape from the sights and sounds and associations of the city; where the eye may feast on the beauties of nature, and where the body and mind may relax and find repose. Therefore, beware of the engineer, the architect and the sculptor, lest their work usurp undue prominence and interfere with the true function of the park.

To erect in a park buildings, bridges, or other structures which are not absolutely essential, or to make them more conspicuous than is unavoidable; to multiply statues; or to introduce unnecessary formal or architectural features, is to defeat the first object of the park, to bring ruthlessly before the mind the image of the city from which one has sought to escape; it is a blunder, an impertinence, a crime.

A park then should consist of natural objects, turf, water, trees and shrubs, arranged by the art and skill of man so as to afford the greatest possible pleasure and enjoyment to the people, with no artificial objects which are not essential to their comfort or convenience.

To which of the arts does this work belong? Is it landscape-gardening? This brings me to a vital question.

Is landscape-gardening one of the fine arts, or is it only a bi-product of the arts, unworthy of the lifelong devotion of a serious mind?

One is almost forced to believe that its professors are ashamed of it. Few of them even call themselves landscape-gardeners any more, but "Landscape Architects," and latterly I have found some classified simply as "Architects." The Oxford dictionary defines an architect as "a master builder; a skilled professor of the art of building, whose business it is to prepare the plans of edifices, and exercise a general superintendence over the course of their erection." I would not quarrel about the name unless there is an idea behind it. I fear that the name is only one of many indications of a tendency to introduce into landscape-gardening a formalism based on architectural lines and principles which, if not checked, will very soon debase and degrade it. Is landscape-gardening one of the fine arts?

It may seem presumption in a layman to express an opinion on this subject; but there is a grain of truth in the proverbial advantage of the looker-on at a game. Ever since I wandered as a lad through the parks and gardens of Europe, I have had a love for landscape-gardening, and have been as closely in touch with it as a layman can be. I believe that landscape-gardening is not only one of the fine arts, but that it is one of the greatest of them, and that it has possibilities of development of which the others are absolutely incapable.

Landscape art — which includes landscape painting and landscape gardening — holds a unique and distinguished position. It is the only one of the arts of design which in the nineteenth century made any progress beyond the achievements of the great artistic periods of history. All of the others have distinctly retrograded. Sculpture is now only the pale shadow of the age of Pericles. The heroic style of painting which deals with religious, historical, and ideal subjects has produced nothing within a hundred years which ranks with the work of the Italian Renaissance.

Architecture as a creative art has ceased to exist. In the place of the mighty builders of the past we now have schools of architecture which formulate rules based on their work; and the best architects of our age are the most successful copyists. When an attempt is made to depart from the formulas of the schools we have such "architectural aberrations" as "L'Art Nouveau," of Paris, or the "Secession Styl," of Vienna.

Landscape painting, however, has made great strides in advance of Salvator Rosa, the best of the Italians, and of the Poussins and Claude Lorrain, the best of the old French schools.

Landscape gardening has made equal progress in the last century and is even more in advance of earlier ages than the Barbizon school of landscape painting is in advance of the Renaissance.

I believe that the explanation of this is not far to seek. A love of nature for her own sake is distinctly modern. Even the greatest of the Renaissance poets show less feeling than those of the Victorian age for the charms and loveliness of natural scenery. It is hardly more than a hundred years since painters first began to see nature as she is and to paint land-scapes truthfully and without artificial features. Until modern times landscape-gardening was modeled exclusively on the old formal gardens of Italy. The terraces which were required on the steep sides of the Italian hills were transplanted to the plains of Versailles and to the gentle slopes of England. You all know the famous old gardens of Italy and the continent. You remember the balustrades; the paved terraces; the straight walks between clipped hedges, and the straight avenues, ending in the inevitable bad statue or silly fountain; the childish surprises of objects which suddenly cover you with spray. If, by chance, you come upon a charming bit of turf, with masses of flowering shrubs and trees not in lines and left to grow untrimmed, you are told — it may be in Italian or German or Spanish or French — that this is the "English Garden"; and you say to yourself, "God bless it!" There is a touch of nature in it.

Now, I ask you, are we to ignore the glorious progress of the nineteenth century and go back to this? Instead of striving to carry landscape-gardening to perfection along the natural lines on which it has made its greatest growth, are we deliber-ately to give up all that the world has gained, and go back for our models to the dark ages of landscape-gardening when it was wholly artificial and unnatural, ages before it had grown to be a fine art? I cannot believe it.

Hence I deprecate the tendency of to-day toward a stiff and unlovely formalism in landscape design. I protest against it because I believe that it will lead to the decadence of a most glorious art which it would reduce to the condition of modern Italian sculpture, mere technique without spirit, a body with-out a soul.

If you think that I exaggerate, I beg you to look over one of the most popular of recent books on landscape-gardening, —

"Gardens Old and New." Turn to the illustration of "formal gardens" and of formal designs; look at them with a thought in your minds of some lovely effects of planting done by nature or by some man who loved her, and tell yourselves honestly what you think of the new-old art. These designs were made with a foot-rule, a straight-edge, and a pair of compasses, and might have been made by an architect, for in his legitimate profession he needs no other tools.

We Americans are a fickle people and are much inclined to change our fashions, not only in dress, but in more serious things. It is this desire for a change for the sake of a change which has prevented the normal development of architecture and stunted the growth of every style in its early youth; but we are also quick to learn and quick to adopt any new thing which is good. The love of the beautiful has only recently begun to develop in this country and the taste of the people is in a formative state and they are just beginning to realize that such an art as landscape-gardening exists. The architects have done much to improve the taste of the dwellers in cities; but only landscape-gardening can reach the great mass of the nation and elevate their taste by teaching them to appreciate the charming things growing wild about them, and ultimately to appreciate everything that is beautiful in nature and art.

A heavy responsibility rests on the leaders in landscape-gardening. They can check the vagaries and inanities which are creeping into it, and which, unchecked, will prove its ruin, and will have a far-reaching effect in giving the nation a false and perverted taste. They, and they alone, can correct its decadent tendencies and maintain the standard which entitles it to rank among the fine arts, and which will lead to its highest development.

Michael Angelo gave up painting in oils and adopted frescos and architecture because they gave a wider scope for his tremendous energies. I sometimes dream that another Michael Angelo will rise among us and that he will find in landscape-gardening the widest scope for the exercise of a mighty creative genius.

In this young country, with its exuberant energy, its increasing wealth, and the development of good taste and a love of the beautiful, the opportunities which the future of landscape-gardening has in store for a great artistic genius seem almost boundless. With vast wealth at his command, and, for materials, the earth, the sky, mountains, lakes, rivers, waterfalls, forests and the flora of the whole earth, and with vistas bounded by the limits of human sight, he can create pictures which will be to natural scenery what the Hermes at Olympia is to the natural man, not copies, but the assemblage of the perfections of nature, beside which the greatest works of other arts will seem as small as the oil paintings despised by Michael Angelo beside the dome of St. Peter's.

If landscape-gardening remains true to its mission, to delight the eye and heart of man by reproducing nature at her best, this I believe to be her destiny, and then architecture will be her willing handmaiden.

INDEX

333

Printed in the United States of America.